TERRA MATER

INSPIRED VERSE

ARUNA PANDEY

Dedicated to Memory: Remembered & Forgotten

Contents

Contents

Contents

Contents

Contents

Contents

Preface

The present verse collection strives to structure patterns of a variety of human experiences. The title of the book is somehow an inevitable one. *Terra Mater* – Mother Earth, is the lap and origin of all humankind. The Earth withholds treasures that nourish and inspire the senses and uplifts the spirit.

All writers go through the process of writing with their own unique set of moods and experiences. Whereas most things are shared, many other aspects of creativity may vary from one person to the other. With reference to my own creative journey, I would like to state that any piece of art is born out of both labour and love for the undertaken course or medium. Poetry, like the other arts, has long withstood the rigours of time and has firmly held ground in a world of radical changes and advanced technologies. The following set of poems have been almost an involuntary outcome of keen observation and intensely lived experiences.

The creative experience has altogether been a roller coaster of emotion, intellectual and spiritual awareness, and social empathies. Many epiphanies have been highlighted and detangled on this exclusive journey of translating experience into words.

This book has been divided into sections for a more distinct and effortless reading experience, and because the topics are various. These verses vary in tone and context and have been categorized accordingly. They may sometimes overlap each other but are convenient for withholding moods, tone and subject matter. Syntax, rhyme, punctuation and other poetical skills have been considered, yet may vary within the volume itself. Each category represents a distinct aspect of the human experience, contributing to the complexities of such phenomena. My choice has been a double-fold, kaleidoscopic vision of humanity at large, ranging from the beauties of nature, social interactions, and special cross-cultural situations. Faith in a higher power – however named, is a recurrent thing in these poems.

My intention is to both entertain through contrast and to introduce myself as the kind of poet that I truly am…life's variety and diversity cannot be missed. At the same time, I believe that our powers are truly endowed upon us by the Almighty, in whichever form we would like to believe in. I begin with a prayer and inspiration from the Muses...

Creativity & observation go hand in hand, no matter how fleeting or unnecessary these observations are - they are part of the larger picture, and it is a delightful exercise to weave the nuances of such phenomenon. In this wonderful journey of expressing and structuring human awarenesses, I must state that I have been rewarded with greater insights into the human predicament. It has been a humbling and enriching experience. Gratitude and contentment are the two purest emotions that touch upon an artist's being. These are the fruits of faith and endurance.

I beg to note that these rhymes are offerings at the feet of the Great Masters who have already, years ago, nourished us with their poetry. The themes, grand and eloquent; homely and humble; the diversity and effects of tone and imagery have all been handed down to posterity, stacked away for our immense benefits. If I resound even once, like the great poets whom I have read and admired - I am blessed and humbled. Like the breeze that is carefree and bountiful, such is the magical presence of the Great Masters of poetry who have touched our lives with their eternal presence.One last observation - Chaos is terrifying and beautiful, and Order is intelligible and comely. The beautiful contradiction lies in the fact that they complement each other. I hope to have combined both aspects of the Universe in this volume.

Finally, I am in awe of the reader who actually breathes life into words by completing the equation on either side. Thank you and happy reading!!

Aruna Pandey,

Jaipur, India

Acknowledgements

In deepest gratitude:

Of what life has offered me

My human race, my powerful gender, my origins...

Our doctors who heal and sustain life and our scientists who enhance our understanding of the Universe

My teachers from nursery through college and university; my job and vocation for allowing me to indulge in what was dear to me—literature and teaching

My students without whom the journey would not have taken place

Friends and colleagues whose presence is incomparable. Like the house that gives shelter or the warmth of a fire in the dead of winter

My unique family - my Parents who are irreplaceable; **my** sisters who complement me in every way; **my** aunts, uncles and cousins, who are a vital force of who I am... the very essence of my being and doing

The next of kin that followed and was the reward—my own children; my unbeatable Partner (spouse) in happiness and struggle—my Mentor

My British and my German connections—friends who are worth the world, rescuing me from the narrowness of geo-cultural boundaries

The very ground I stand on today, the present, alive and well in the midst of calamities untold…

My unknown future that patiently awaits my arrival—this very moment, that I may bow down in gratitude

Thank you,

Aruna

The Muse

A life force; an inspiration...

A companion and a stern master

1. Holy Be to You: The Muses

An inspiration is a reverend Deity
Or vice versa if you will...
Song & dance and memory
The Arts and Poetry all Entwined
No hubris now of gifts
That have been endowed
On one so special and yet not so.
Superior is another force
An energy all rarefied
Bow down, in humbleness
Around: 'Tis this that makes
You proudly stand and
Spin the world around.
The dance does touch the ground
The song the air; the warriors'
Frames the Linnet's song
The drums of war or warbled
Flute of lovelorn souls
Departed now
Separated from each other

Basking in another glow
Denying world, friend or foe.
Lift the world out of its
Slumber or the mighty wind
To curb: Stop the flames
From fleeing on towards
The wondrous forests shorn
Teach oh Muse to follow
Chords of Rhyme or Reason
Dance and Song that never
Would exist without the balance
Or the fortitude required to
Blow the horn of Plenitude.

2. A Prayer

Lift:

The world out of its slumber— Not in peaceful rest it lies,
Anxious, restless, never glad—
One eye open; fretful lies and secret

Shake:

Dear Muse, and blow into the dying embers
That are only sick aglow.

Teach:

The mighty wind to curb,
Stop the angry flames to dare
From flaring on towards
The wondrous Forests burning
Down, soon shorn of handsome glory.
Decline, *deprive, de-*
Mystify, all things that so confuse..
Teach your children then to follow
Truth and honest chords —of Reason and of Rhyme.

Tell them:

Dignified, respectable and dutiful,
Are the purest forms, of Art and Poetry:
Dance and Song would ne'er

Exist without great balance, all-inclusiveness and gen'rous
fortitude.
Remind us:
Proud but humble in your gait
You must show to be;
Be worthy of the name you have
Bow down in all humility to justify your
Sanctioned space—
***Blessed** with wings, now you may*
Soar, and blow the Horn of Plenitude.
The world awakened thus will
Make glad; ready to take on the show,
With beating heart and honest eyes.

The Earth: Terra Mater

Our Earth is the surest and safest way to know why and who we are…it is the finite within the infinity: a microcosm.

3. MOTHER

Confront yourself in these towering trees
Dense with time and struggle
To survive. Shaggy now and shaggier still in all-assuming
Brow. No fear of any other, save
The sky which may horrendous throw its rage to fell down
In its own chosen way. Merciless and full
Of spite, only though when heavy clouds overbearing seize the space
As dark as Death or anything, and anger in its breath that's hot and cold
Both in extremes:
Fearful, shuddering in the wake; the eager foliage hides away
From wrath and horror of the storm which may ravish
And destroy the century's-old existence of these ancient forests—
The storm is over; it's done it's job;
The tree breathes heavy with the thought—
With apprehension of what had happened it feels
For roots—intact and firm—oh, thank the Lord!
Now thinking next; it rolls along its limbs to feel
In pain acute but strong. The feeling's good—its being
Secure; deep inside but something different—
What was it? An altered vision—the sky was gone

The green stretched wide; emerald, dewy, mossy, furry.
Disoriented was this state, the tree was tired; it grew dark
With sunshine on the following morn' everything would be okay…
The night was deep and long.. stubborn in its ways..
A breeze did grow; fresh and ruffled up the leaves that
Seemed to whisper into the very rings of the seasoned
Trunk—everything seemed close at hand.
Where was the sky—it was not seen
Anywhere! The grounded tufts with wet grass still
Were the things that could be seen. The tree—it
Gasped with bated breath and knew how terrible indeed,
Had been the storm.
Some thinking went into the
Air. The tree it breathed some breaths so rare—
As if to stimulate its mind—A speck of consciousness spoke
Up, to tell, in eagerness, the Tree: "The Storm, the Dark and Evil Guy, blew
Right through 'n' through your branches— so erect so regal.
Still tall and noble, bent you are; perhaps forever—the sky is there for everyone
But more and more the one you'll see is the
Emerald green of grass; Velvet carpet you've not seen
In years of looking up toward the
Watery blue and crimson red; the stormy black
And pleasant grey—your head held high for much too long,

Bend down with grace and now enjoy the glowing embers of the earth.
Befriend the Earth that's held you warm, alive;
Deep roots inside Her dark brown honest
Womb—no complaints of having stood: Haggard,
Outworn in such perpetual state—Mother Earth will hold you still—
It's only you who will one day: tired, weary with cares
And age—choose to leave and crack the ground
With weight thrown down; Uprooted there for Timber:
Precious, eternal, rare.

4. Gratitude

I'll never wish for life itself to live again
For me. I love to think of stumbling oft'
On every path I took—a chance to look
On sky and ground and every living thing around—
The trees and stones, they'd look at me
I certain was good blessed, to have their
Company.
I hope I gave some goodness back —
I sure was blessed with many; it is not easy
To express, the gratitude that lives through,
Each day that's given as a gift from Heaven..
With reverence I do say these words—in
Humbleness to stand.

5. Terra Mater

— The sky is there to humble us;
The wind blows through unkind —
Invisible it gives us breath to live
And to survive.
The elements are but unique and help us stand the ground.
It's the Earth receiving still, in any good or bad;
Condition we may find ourselves,
For want of this and that—
A cautious word, a helping hand that missed
The Moment's anxious tear. Go rock and roll, forget all cares—
Fall strong into your Mother's lap; Fondness of the Earth does bear
Ourselves forever dear. The warmth, the hug, the constant touch
Helps to revive; rejuvenate; the battered, weathered soul—
That searched, here there and everywhere.

6. Dig Deeper

The earth is bare just lying there
For you to unravel treasures rare
It is earthy honest brown
Take it as a gift of God
Before you take onto the world.
Mother Earth she's rightly called
Baring all for humankind
Taking all unto her bosom
Nurturing, challenging, daring
Each one for the rough and tumble that
Awaits.
Dig you deeper, faster
Eager— layer upon layer
To discover rarest gems and
Gold of glowing hue.
When you're tired sleepy
Worn: slip into Her welcome folds;
Rocking in Her gentle arms,
Mother Earth will give us all
Unconditional mirth and laughter.
Deeper, faster and with
Care— take good heed

Of what God gave you
All for free: a paradise with
Toil and work is even better
Than with where you drift in leisure
Ease to stare with nothing to
Look forward to; save for Dusk to
Follow Day; Night eager then to
Bustle through into its well allotted
Place in the scheme of smoothest
Time where rules are naught
And aimless moments
Pile on to make a half- lived day.
Pray in gratitude and love
For the Earth that's everywhere.
Not for Adam for the Sin
But truly just a better place
To gently firmly guide
Our way.
Patient, still and going round
The Sun to redefine the space
We have a new one everyday
To be born and grow again.

Of Time

Only time will tell how well we've done… if Time is really how we strive to know it.

7. Time?

If me and my limbs could travel that far
Where the mind does of its own accord,
Filling gaps with rivulets of this and that,
How happily my soul would sing, and I would bring
Back many friends of the lovely past.
Every second's a fleeting thing—where it
Goes we do not know; maybe it's a good thing though
To move forward, eager; covering many places
Many people, we will love mostly tomorrow.
Recover not your covered ground; your lovely
Mind to ponder at: the once lived thing is gone forever;
The one awaiting: seize it now—
Embrace, observe, reflect, collect—
The beauties of the here and now!

8. Jealous

Time is jealous of itself—
It cannot stand upright;
It leans forwards to disgrace
The footsteps left behind.
Time is hasty, proud and careless;
Doesn't care for the here and now
It's the future always there to make
It run just everywhere!
Time is kind—it heals and nurses
Every sorrow, tear and gloom; seldom fails,
To make it go away; It bathes us with
The light of day and soothes us with
It's nightly, sober charms.
Time is dark, moody, pensive…
It knows not how to move or stay—
A Chatterbox, a Clown, a King that
Rules the Earth and makes it spin!

9. Time Again

If time were something
You could stop
From travelling near and far
We'd have the sun and moon together
What a ghastly thing to do.
If time did wander here and there
Far far away from man and demon
Where would we be
We could not know.
Time is fleeting; time is slow
We're almost done or not
We know.
It gives us freedom to make our plans
To delve and dive and swim and breathe.
I hate to say that now I know
What it is to do and go—
When one moment takes the other
By the collar, by the neck
Telling it that its time
To go and join the past
Forever

10. Let's Get Back To

Let's get back to
Keeping distance in our minds
Revering God's ways of time and space
Read along and you'll know why.
With the rising of the sun, the moon
Does quietly go away — it is true for
Anyone and anything that
Follows all the natural laws
What men have done is big
Shame: have altered everything possible from
Day and night; violating all
Regularity,
Distance can no longer hold
Us faithfully bound to one dear place
Our greedy desires do unfold
With shameless possibilities
The ongoing trends of being
Everywhere all at once — one step taken
Then another and another
And then falling to the wheel
That goes on it seems forever.
So bent we are in following

The path before as its so even
Smooth and joyous in it's speed
So fast and slick it's like a dream
Until it's over and we discover
The illusion, the hollow, fretful shape of
Lives.
It is too too just far away—
To regret with rewards
Too late it is for finer things
That would have gladly come our way
Had we understood the game
That invention, discoveries do play
Upon our minds and souls do reach
Away from all that's good and helpful
To mankind till evermore.

11. Time

Doesn't always have to be here and gone
Something to feel sorry for or
Regret
Just because it flows and runs
Falls and crashes on the shore
Too massive to embrace our sight
Powerful, full of delight. Only from a distance though—
Don't venture to get very close
It's there with you in joy and
Fear.
A comfort not a nervous thing
To make you think of it all the
The while— let it go for it to be
A friend in need— a friend indeed.

Of Words

Despite our word banks teeming with expressions… spilling over …we fall short of communication.

12. Anonymous

How I love the word Anon
If it actually is a word. No
Matter if it hasn't a form
It's good for me in any way.
Anon does give me freedom to
Do it in just my own peculiar way;
I shan't give others a chance to
Peep and ponder; pry or play
Around with my decent, mad,
Wild and Fickle; grey and white
Identity.
Thank God for this blank and
Pure; white and Sacred Space
That's there — no visas or no
Passports are required to buy oneself that
Heavenly Space. It comes for free
Along with will and courage.
To pass unknown, forgotten
Free.
Identities are for mostly those
Who strive for goals achievable;
Of tangibles and sensual treats

For medals, trophies and the like.
Whoever cares for quite just nothing
But to breathe the freedom of
The state of Being and the
Success of being always Fair
Will turn to what we call negation
Of the self---Anon.

13. A Scent Divine

I love the smell of pages from
A book that sits on a dusty shelf
From some past of someone
Who bought, read, savoured, and put it back
For someone else like me to take
It down one leisurely day with
Fervour and delight at the
Hoary passing of all the shaggy
Years gone by into shadows dark and grey
Coming back from inside the book
That's now dusted; pages open
In my receiving hands.

14. Every Cloud Has A Silver Lining…

Phrases, sayings are e'er so witty,
Well thought out and very pretty,
To the sound and to the mind,
To the heart and to the soul.
One too many; thanks a ton;
Goodness gracious; go to hell.
Fear no friend and trust no foe;
All that glitters is not gold—
Ignorance is bliss; fair-weathered friends;
Handsome is
What handsome does;
Water seeking its own level;
Leaving someone high and dry;
Contradictions, indications, of
Many kinds we come across:
Not excluding complex dreams ,
Scary, pleasant, or just funny.
Live long indeed but not
Inside, a Fool's Paradise:
You'll regret, sleeping through life's

Splendid moments all too
Fleeting— like the sturdy dandelion
That will take the weakest breeze to carry and blow
Away to glory
Vanishing, scattering everywhere.
Not to be gathered any more
By human hands or nature's care.
Every cloud a silver lining
Has—to help, consider, perk up
So many awaited sweet delays: The hour is darkest before
The dawn; light and shadow
Play along...in almost sacred union.
Think not of fruits, or just rewards
For endeavours that did fall
Along life's earnest pathways:
To save you from further disgrace;
A waste of life; of human skill;
Of doing nothing, wanting all.

The Primary Glory

Every year, Nature dresses up

to awaken, to infuse and to surprise.

Repeating itself and yet shocking us into variousness

15. The Twelve Months of the Year

January is a month that has
A full blank stare and no rewards
Just the faintest memory
Of last year's Christmas, faded now
With the turn of just one day
And bygones must indeed
Be gone.
February turns a restless turn;
Low the voices; tremors mild
To life's erratic, pounding
Beats.
We now remember that we
Have something more than
Just to wonder, wish and
Watch the fast and glowing Melting snow.
Come March and it's a sad
Affair; with growling winds and bursting pops
Together they do go against
Pure happiness and the chance to do
What we should return to too

However melancholy it seems
It's only good for latent bliss:
The calm before the storm,
Let's say; because for sure
The reason is that beauty lies
Within the womb of sternest
Temper; darkest gloom.

◦

April is the key to many,
Many apprehensions; fluttering
Hearts, forgotten things;
To set aright and forge ahead
With Duties of another kind
All demanding our keenest
Ever, intense and loving, good attention.
May brings ease and sun and
Flowers that spell some kind of
Respite from gloomy thoughts
And worthless dreams that
Never will become for real.
Be you merry; be you gay—
Be you strong and straight and
Play— round and round the month of May.
June is somewhat heavy ladened
Maybe with summer's lazy notion
That everything will one day
Be fine and we will gather into

Merry, easy, Jubilee.
With the buzzing of the Bees
And the droning of the wasps
Nature heavy and despot.
A maiden fair shall duly follow
The path that you have chosen
Borrowed.
The month that follows is
July— a very just and proper
Fellow— friendly, big and burly, kind:
Embracing all our stupid
Worries of this and that, that's
Very crazy.
Come August— do you scent the lovely
Smells of flowers
Stream aflowing…
Can you see, I'm sure you can;
The laughing mermaids, joining
Hands, in confidence that
The best is now and better
Still, tomorrow morn.
Come September, all your woes have tidied up in one lonely huddle
The orchestra of delightful music
Floats across azure blue skies.
The air is bright; the air is right;
Sprinkling forth a heady

Fragrance of romance and Cupid's bow aiming here, there
And Everywhere.
October is the real Queen
Of all the months gone before: Steady and Supreme.
Eternal balance is the goal —
Striking hard and mellow stern
The eye on her who bargains
Life with death or vice versa
Or unexpected or aggrieved
The giant lady of the Lamp.
Wisdom, grace and the right
Degree of show and pomp.
November in her righteous mood
Stands in judgment erect and
True.
She has promised not to hurt
Friend or foe; or any other
Creature fair or not so good.
She is noble in her mind and
Heart for every single situation.
Wiping off the faintest notion
Of gloomy thoughts and
Apprehensions.
The month that marks the
End is indeed a friend— a friend in need
Of festive cheer and the mark of
Jesus Christ.

Fair, serene; pure and pious
Lovely and demure December
But sure and steady of the
Jobs that may be over—
Done, despite the fact that
Not much time is spent in
Doing something else.
Choose the one that you love
Most— it's up to you and your
Endeavours that match themselves
To one another— I too think
That it is true that we do love
Most the month in which we came
Into the world alone
In other words, let's just say,
The month that we
Were Born, that chosen day.

16. The Rose

The Rose is but the only flower
that abundance, cunning custom, has not staled.
That's known for beauty, passion, colour, power
With centuries of keen desire for much the very same.
Artists, poets spin out tales of woe, love in earnest throes
Tales that travel far and wide; writhing hearts and minds
Alike; pleasing and appeasing both, the mass of Human-
Kind. Passionate, tender and forlorn much to the echo sounds
Firm and emerald green; smooth the stem; with spiky thorns that grow along
To guard the weary, careless traveler, from plucking quick the reddest one
In selfish wrong reward—God's perfection and creation; beautiful and strong
Toil and beauty grow together without rest, until the rugged journey's done.
Noah's Ark so bold and fair
Admitted those who came in pairs.

17. The Daffodil

Oft' has this merry Marigold
Been mistaken for another name
Especially by us who have had
A glimpse of so many others just like them.
They give you time and wisdom to
Understand with all the knowledge at
Your hand, to know and recognise the
Colour, shape and texture, they carry
Springtime through, banishing the cold of
Winter and the snowy blues.
You cannot miss; you shouldn't so
The long smooth stem that disappears
With such good grace and modesty
At the start of the flower's lovely, hanging, firm and sunshine head.
Look not in haste or you'll regret, the leaves that shine
Without the Sun: Slender, bigger, longer, smoother,
Firmer, than your pink and outstretched palm
Spread gracefully for the breeze to catch
A fragrance of eternity—of life come back
For so much so as the prelude to the Organ
Is; so is the dainty, head-hung-low;

Springtime's lovely golden humble, all-time
Favourite, Poet's and the Artist's flower.

18. Carnations

These savoury, pink and pretty flowers don't ever come
Alone. They are bunchy munchy crunchy as they look
Like frosted cakes. Unique in colour, shape and size—
Whoever thought of laying them down only by the
Yonder grave, was in a hurry to get done
With something without love for God's gift of
Shapes and petals; stalks and perfect bloom—
To make it look as if these were meant to be
Laid side by side with someone's Tomb.

19. Poppies

The Poppy is the only flower
That blows in thousands in
The wind.
One would say that it is just
As pretty as another of its
Breed.
Yet no poet has ever written
Some lines in praise of these: Why is it so
That none so far has given colour, brushstrokes to
A crowded Poppy field blowing gently
Surely, mesmerising the fainting Air.
Buttercups and dandelions
Heather and the mulberry bush
Escape the poet's eye but with the
Poppies of the field, the story
Is not known. It is as if in a
Trance that for a fleeting second,
The sight of these and we're rooted at the spot;
The next instinct is followed
By a clear decision to quickly
Quit and run.
There is a distance that exists

Between these poppies and the Man
Who never would approach or
Stop to really look or inhale
The floating, breathless air
Around.
In fact when passing by a red and glorious
Poppy Field, the mass of colour;
A monochrome; Hurts the eyes and makes
A mess inside your mind…
There is no desire to stand
Or savour: to look on or to inhale
The strongest, strangest fragrance / smell
Of the Flower World.

20. Crocuses

What beholdings of the earth
Do meet the eye one afternoon,
When on your walk you do espy
Crocuses: like a bed of snow;
An afterthought that Nature had,
Laid out for our souls to lie
Upon — heaven-sent comforts
In return of strife and struggle; wintry
Woes and icy snow— melt away to nought
And sweet dissolve into the breeze
That's come to breathe new life,
New powers and new strengths
Into all that had dried up and had mournful shrivelled,
Gone: Into some unknown terrain....
It is the vision, not the scene
Of colours spread across the
Earth.... Or sky...wrapping up
In purple-white human dreams,
Divine delights... of yesteryears
Or present glows; or much the future
In its throes of passionate and
Of fleshly or of worldly gains.

Look upto this— the flow and promise…
The run of Nature, never dulled by
Grey routine, or the need to follow such,
Usual, straight; the accustomed
Path… leading much to what has
Yet, for centuries, gone on before.
What sweetness blows from a
Single mindedness; single tune;
There's music in some known pursuits;
Desire and pleasure good contained,
Brimming, leaning, leaving not
The form, the space, the even
Gait. Such Godliness resides inside
Devotion to a norm; the rules
Of Nature running through the
Channels of Eternity.

21. Routine

There is a certain majesty in
Dried up barks and twigs that
Show their bareness proud
And tall, in grief of leaves, once
Green and young, now shed
And disappeared—
No fault of any else but that
Which constant rules the Universe: Routine.
The meekest light does filter through
And spreads a smile across the face
Of Nature willing to restore the meagre looking place.
A liquid thing seems all afloat—the absent river flowing
Now, around the objects one sees through: it seems
Transparent water; sometimes crystal, sometimes hazy,
A dreamy state to be in one—yet with the rush of children now,
And buses going off to school, shouting, screaming; red cheeks
And horse-like power— bringing back the real of Life; I smile
and
March ahead.

22. Energy

The wind does blow
Comes not the snow
But storm and clouds
Black with thunder
All asunder. Chasing out the
Feeble, now meek wind; that thought itself
Sovereign in its powers of use
Of energy and mighty motions
Of the landscape's famous poles;
Sarcastic: Tall and proud
Dancing (not the Daffodils);
But man-created
Whirring still—
the haughty doughty
Erectest WINDMILLS.

23. Freedom: A Dream

Written in a dream:
I'm a cloud that does surpass
The highest mountains and the
Grass that looks greener on the other side:
I have a view of many things
And I could tell stories of wide and far
With distance by my side to see
With clarity of what goes on.
People happy sad or gay; running children off to school;
Animals lazy in the Zoo, or
Poppies lousy in the self-created fragrant air
Brilliant red, azure blue sky,
Rocking, rolling without care
The farmer given up his worries
At one with earth and sky alike.
But don't believe a tale twice told—
It may not be the only one to
Know or learn about these darling poppies RED,
Nodding waving spontaneously
Azure blue-sky above; dancing in the fields
Below, the brown earth nurturing tenderly.
If you don't know what I do mean;

Tell it then to everyone and
Let one who is wise unfold
The truthfulness of all that seems
Guarded yet from all you see.

24. Dualities

Robin redbreast at my window
Chirpy chilling in the winter
Air— I can see the beating of
Its tiny heart
Throbbing gently, steady rhythm;
And the motion of its eyes
Small yet glassy; vibrant wise.
The twiggy branches of the trees
Or the bushes spread out wide;
Laden white with purest snow
Give a backdrop so amazing
That you'd think you'd ever know….
Until you spy a holly bush
Standing out in sharpest eye
Glistening green and shocking red
The thorny firmness of the leaves does prick the eyes
And the berries soothe them next—with their smoothy earnest red.
Another combination of the lion and the lamb
Strength and gentleness do so
Coexist: harmonious, balanced
And forlorn.

25. The Heat

It's rather hot and I do know
That this will overpower my
Soul— not allowing me
To follow, gently chirping birds'
Twitter: Or the rustling of the dried-
Up leaves upon the
Tree, waiting for the gusty
Shower to drench it just
One last time more.
The rain will make me glad again
Of seasons that do come and go
But takes away the lovely sounds
That sink deep into the muffled beats
Of hateful dust and treacherous heat.
Take and give or give
And take- you can't have both
Your cake and eat it too...
Simple wisdom, simple Faith
In universal facts to know
And march past all that's there to gain
With focus on the bigger cause
Never slackening, never a pause

To quit the Truth or Nature's
Laws
Is the wise man's rule; the fools
Despair;
Forgetting that what gives will take back quietly the first— You
may travel far and wide
Till the vast and vaguest
Shore of emptiness and morrow's doom,
Never to find again your place
That you had boldly left
Behind.
Gratitude will take you far
Into a realm of constant bliss
Where you're not yearning,
Heading for: things that are
Of no use at all.
Breathe the air around you;
Stand, erect so you don't bow
To things that are beyond
Your grasp.
Life too often teaches us
A day too late; a day too early
Of the moving of the
Earth and the Sun's
Diurnal round. Catching
Us so unaware of what's to
Follow; what takes place:

Much beyond the grasp of
Men.

26. The New Dawn

It's a flush that is unique
The scarlet colour on your face
It's time to anchor onto one who's there
For you here and everywhere you go.
Made in Heaven
Let's not deny
The dreamy texture
Of this time he
When two souls just fuse
Into one: ever searching
For the rightest time
When destiny does engage
With passion and desire
To holy matrimony still.
Sound of church bells all around
Chiming to the happy ground Air and sky and the Divine
Echoed through the forest
Green and dense; the creatures there
Do stand still to justly acknowledge the passionate play:
The heavenly human theatre.
Mantras chanted by the dozen
Overlapping one for the other

In incessant full throated ease
By Pundits who are gathered
Splendid, duly there.
And the heady sound of Conch
Revel rejoice forever more to mark the
End and mark the pause
Of childhood grown up big and
Strong — in it's bid to be
Right there to mark off
The dawn of another time; another day.
Heaven's blessings from above
Can be seen without a trace
Of gaps and spaces the wanton air
Does bear.
Endless blooms and fragrant
Blossoms scatter all along the Fresh and special
Ever eager; bright and pretty, Silent, coy, the haloed visage
Of Nuptial softness and delay.
Time stands still in moments
Pure— distilled, sparkling
Like white wine.
Crystal clear ; trembling still but
Without the fear that dogs our steps:
Of future ills do lovers
Know how to Thrive.

27. The Power of Grey

The cleanest slate of palest grey
Is laid outside my window's glass
Thank you for these—French they're called.
Just today — I think my heart was waiting for
This purest colour so divine.
Where whiteness with a fleck of black
Lay down together, glad afloat:
In the most perfect embrace.
First, I looked and it was plain
Dimmest light of sun not there:
Not the sun gone down to set
But snuggled in the whitest clouds
Not really visible but expanded into
The awesome grey of all around.
This summer has been very fair
It gave us muted shades of heat
A day or two of howling winds
To just remind us of who it was
Mornings bleak but up and rising
Afternoons slightly confused
But gathering dusk would seem to spread quietly
Across the sky with desired, lovely

Hues each day—different almost every time.
Delightful but with hidden pangs
Of something certainly amiss
Then to break into a fury that's
Not new to one who's lived
Long enough to know that
Here, on the outskirts of the sand
Summer rushes into these
Outbursts almost every Eve.
As if in self responding mood
The wind oscillates between the two—
Slow and fast and very wild
Until it gives in to its own Design.
Changes motion on becoming
Sullen and afraid of its own ruinous fury to
And maybe to the chirping birds' soulful
Cries: "Please be rested, if
You are Shelly's West Wind
Spirit fair—control yourself;
Another Day, let pass away
Without plunder, without distress
If such we mortals may request".
Nature listens to one who's honest
Genuine in appeal—no selfish gain
Or mean revenge.
Almost quiet, like an empty Church that's haloed
The Heavens bring forth a

Calm again of different kind.
I look back to the scene once more:
To my delight and quick discover—
A blush of gorgeous red indeed!
From the corners of some roofs;
Dwellings of the human race outlined
Pencil-like along an Artist's hands;
Slowly spreading God knows to
Where, how, and when and why.
Don't be sad or try to know
What forces of the wind does blow
Through trees and boughs; what
Path it follows; left alone
It is your friend; gives us
Energy and transforms
To one pulsating giant Form
The silent tomb of
Heaven and Earth.

At Large

The tools to recognise the supreme realities are scattered in the world around us. They teach, we learn; they are redefined, so we teach.

28. Sisters

Sisters are a dreadful lot
If they cross the line of two—
Three is crowd and complication
Four is better in some ways: each has one.
Five is just a nightmare and an evil, magic
Number—very scary never humble
Puffing on the air for having
Always much around. In a bid to have it all
None remains to look around.
Maybe it's a better thing to be gifted with
Just one; so that each one has one still —
Together they are only two.
May not Fate just misunderstand what
I say here in desperation—I wish for
Luck and love for all- the ragged jagged fair or not;
This my genuine consideration.
I am the eldest and so have felt in many ways
Privileged than the rest of them; however much they might
Have tried, they've given into my ways and rights.
Better still I'd like to say, privileges are double fold
In the fact that I remain lazy and without a care

I have an army that takes good care in times of trouble and despair.
I will now revise my faith in having four;
Me the fifth; i guess it works well both
Ways; I may choose every now and then
Yet for sure they never can- as I would be there each time
With age and number on my side. I didn't know this when I began
To say I'm unhappy about the five
And that is why I reasoned out by writing
Lines to understand—such is the beauty of
A Verse.

29. Fed Up

I am now fed up
With life living it the way I have
No regrets but enough of what lays in the
Past; I want a space yet
Unexplored to stumble and
Maybe get caught by unknown
Dangers; who knows for sure
Whether I will see the end of the
Journey and the Path that yet will come to me.
I pray and know that God
Will grant this wish for sure:
I'm half afraid that it might be
Something that's not meant for me;
But saturation of this kind
I never knew existed till it
Really came— I know just
How exhausting it can be.
I still look forward though
Apprehensive, of the options
That might be placed right in front
Of me, and I would be then,
At a loss to decide— which is which; that's good for me.

Boredom is a really sad
State of Affairs. It doesn't
Necessarily have to be
But generally, it always is.
Try not to be bored as very soon
It has you in its grips and is
Called by different names:
Depression, madness, sadness
Of a special kind that is far from
Being special and also good
At the same and equal time.
I like the gardener with his spade
With his hook and with his rake
It looks as if he didn't care
For anything except the plants
And trees and bumble bees.
The cook's face is full of glee
At what she's doing baking basting
Cutting chopping washing
Cleaning— everything that goes into
A perfect meal for more than two.
The Maid is happy every time
To work inside another's home
She roughs it out for you and me
So that she can keep a home
And the children all intact.
The postman is a man whose

Only happiness lies in other peoples
Cheerful faces at receiving long
Awaited; messages and other news.
I like the doctor in the ward
Whose stethoscope around
His neck does hang whose very
Presence cheers and instils
Confidence in every man,
Woman Child Grandma, Pa
I like the Nurse all uniformed
Tipping sideways for a glance
Of her patient's health and mood
With reassuring smiles and
Words for her to spend the livelong Day.
I like to see a baby snuggling
Close unto her mother's bosom
With no knowledge of what goes on
Outside the fragrance of her body.
It's cruel to expect someone
To be just like you.
Just as cruel it must be to
Have you be like someone else.
So, spare the rod and spoil
The child without the fear
Of anything. Children are
Won through tolerance of their own intolerance
For you and me and he and her.

30. The Guardians

Doctors there are far too many
Some are plump and short, I say;
And on the rebound, dark and grey.
Jollywolly, tumbly grisly—all of this and
Many more: with hunched back from overwriting
Or to slice an organ here or stitch
Together back in pairs—the layers of injured
Sinew, muscle, tissue—all seeking to rebind, repair.
There's the one we oft must meet
She means a lot to us because
She gives us joy with priceless gifts—
A bubbly boy or gurgling maiden
Walking talking dolls so cute
To hold onto our lives forever.
The one we meet with casual boredom
Rattling forth a list of woes,
Is the one with spectacles perched on his noble wobbly nose
It seems forever. He doesn't look up to see
Us there; he knows us all without the need to stand and stare
The meds are listed e'en before we've finished
Speaking fast the symptoms so many in number
With the parting, "right we are!"

The one who will treat us for
A grousy mood and utmost care
For things insignificant or not
Droopy eyes and swollen hands
No ailment save the deep despair
For living on in this wide world
With no one there to ever care.
His eyes are kind with a clear hint
Of madness gleaming now and then
Because of too much learning how
To manage, treat and banish then
The keen despair their patients have.
Beware, he may become so stern
Throwing caution to the winds
He may scold in thunderous voice
That you have not been sharp and merry.
Many will not see him though
Even once in all their time
It is an option that we care about
Our feelings and our trust in man
And science that says it has the cure.
God bless docs for what they do
No matter that they are who
They are: each one so different from
The other—in appearance; in approach;
Much resigned to bringing hope, and cheer and
Sometimes stress—on account of diagnosis right and false

That is serious, sometimes fatal.
It's not rosy all the time
Things go wrong and
Some don't mind; some fall
Prey to constant weeping
But the comfort's always there
The young doctor, walking briskly
To share your grief and pain
Alike; Apprehensions brought along
With too much google and advice
From others who they think they
Know: how and what to do along
Much as the doctor maybe there
With deepened brow and buzzing mind
Thinking on the whole day long
Of other treatments, other measures
To help and cure all in time.
I've said enough to praise the crew
And there are some things more than this
I write.
I remember well and knew—but it is not the
Moment now to talk of this and that
Together—let's all take a bow
And thank ;
All our doctors, past and present;
Thanks for saving, pulling through
The pain and misery of the suffering

With good knowledge of what ails
And will further keep us well.
My father was a doctor too
Now in Heaven, skies all blue
Greenest meadows do await
The treading of his humble feet;
The air so fortunate to feel,
The grazing of his wise old cheeks;
A smile so simple; gaze so tender—
It filters through to many hearts;
Still: in the deepest layers of gloom.
A doctor never dies at all: he lives on
Forever: beating in the warmest
hearts of
People he has left behind.
Those —children, old and young alike
Frail but healed, the troubled souls
Whom he gave forth with loving hands
Whatever needed and required
To heal and save from
Pain and suffering; Torture sheer
In exchange of life not death
For now and forever more.
I am indebted to all who are
The Noble Tribe who do replace
God indeed here on this
Earth to save us from the final

Doom.
It gives me cheer; it gives me heart
To ponder on what I have gained
Through you to others; others who
Have received, gladly little that i do
To carry on in spirit of values that are dear to me.
A rare Inheritance for me—Fortune of a special kind
Not to mention long-life strength and
Brilliant insight and Repose.
Dearest doctors, we beseech:
Take great care of yourselves, do:
Don't forget you're human too;
You need nutrition, care and rest
You have a family waiting there
Forget your worries, toil and fret;
Go back to them with all your love.
You also have the right to marry; have
Lovely children; sleepless nights;
Not on account of service prompted
Shrill the call from hospital
But to awake to your very own
Happy snores and wailing cries;
Nappies, bottles, midnight smiles.
Do not miss out on all this fun and frolic—
Just as others whom you cherish,
We do care and love you too.

31. Stop Wondering

The day was nigh the
Sun was high up
In the sky—
Birds of a feather flocked together
In their daily acts of pleasure.
I'd done my job of here and there
Reaching everywhere
On time. I was happy
So to say— but something wrong inside my mind.
Lunch time over; tea time too
Things were streamlined-perfect good;
Almost done and time to go
Home again, but
What was this— I felt so out of
Place it seemed to me, to really be
The end of the world in
Deepest, darkest yonder sea.
I tried with all my might I swear Couldn't place my
apprehension:
Counted all the things I'd done
And had to do tomorrow morn'
I saw no gap at all, no hint

As to why I felt this way
Of this state of misery.
Dinner over, nagging still,
Music wafting through the lawn
No emotions or regrets but
Heavy, fluttery troubles in my heart
I still was sad; embittered
And confused—the reason why,
It only came to me when
I, just before I went to bed,
Picking up my toothbrush
Once again, or so I thought—
Green and dry and not yet wet,
Realising all at once—
That I'd not brushed
My teeth that day!!
So when you're doing well
But feel that things aren't happy as
They seem— think of this then
First of all and maybe this
Is what it was.
See how all these little
Things come together
And combine to make up all
That's true and happy —
Never
Ever blame another for the

Ever changing mood or
Weather— it is in essential
Acts of going through the little
Basic bits of habits. Pleasure
Then it is to do all that is
Important too;
Useful, and does lead the way
To a splendid hard-earned day.
A green canopy is the best
Umbrella that saves all
From the thunder and the rain but can't be bought.
It takes years and years to grow that way
And defeats all human endeavours

Not the Least of Places

Every place has its earnestness and its peculiarities that make it unique. In its uniqueness it connects to the similitude of things.

32. Camden Town 1993

It was a time when cheer and glee
Were very seldom not together
Even in a dire event, they coexisted like true fellows
In the grey and hidden shadows.
Camden Town is not too far
From its fatherland the city
Of London. Some people like to call it suburbs
Different from the towns in that
Were scattered all along.
Newtons they were called at last
No better name than true to face.
So, Camden then becomes
The final destination of the subway and the bus
That rumbles through the cobbled streets and smoothest tracks.
It has a fresh appeal no doubt
The air is lighter to breathe somehow
Although you can see the soot climb up
Into the gathering of the clouds—
The blue of sky is hardly there
But you can see it in your mind
For there's so much gladness
All around.

Best of both
Worlds, I would say;
Fuming fretting not from habit
But from the knowledge that
It stays with labour and the rising
Times of today.
This town is London in its prime
Shorn of indifference, race or crime
It's clearer in the bearing
Of beginners who do find
Shelter, approval and embrace.
The rain is gone and people still do march along
With fresher smiles
That the crispy air with sun and cool do bring together.
The scene is a painting from
The Artist who nobody has seen
At labour. The spread out canvas mixes hues and kindly faces
With homely smells from down the
Bakers'.
Shiny cars so smoothly gone into the disappearing act
Of humble jobs and families
Who wait for arrival of the
Handsome men and giggly girls
One with a pink or blue umbrella—
Pretty someone standing at the corner now
Freckled face, dewy eyes,
Long blonde hair with reddest lips.

Two young friends who have avowed
To stick in rain and hail together
There's another shouting loud
To sell her little trinkets and umbrellas: "April showers — come and grab one before there's none!"
What is this but not Divine
God's good world in utmost
Action, thought and care.
The sparkling rainbow come out now
Arching right across the town
Above beyond and not so near.
Brilliant hues of vibgyor—
Overlapping without sound or
Without the slightest hurry.

33. In Eibelstadt, Bayern, Germany

I switched off the lights
Tonight: As always done before
It's time to close one's eyes
And dream of this and that—
That time of day to fast retire;
It's comforting but now the shadows
Confront you in a loneliness—
In custom and in pensiveness,
I so retired between the layers of an eiderdown
That keeps us warm on winter days
Not promising however, to bless
With sleep, the lying down, as vain I did aspire.
My eyes looked out yet once again
Upon this land of beauties rare;
The dark tonight was different; restless—
Not pitch black as mostly seen;
I wondered at a pale green light that filtered through the curtains—
Sheer net and lace exquisite: never failing
To appeal, but light shone in

Like ne'er before and sparkling;
Rather green— iridescent—
I cared not—I thought ahead— another night
To think again of so much from
The present, future and the past
A never ceasing song!!
Distraction grew; the lighted curtains glowing through:
They drew attention once again
I had no other way to go, save draw
The curtains much aside to see
What made it glow.
No wind did blow; no unforeseen
Characters in sight.. a gloom and
Brightness both together—
An artist's painted masterpiece !
The Master's rusty bicycle
Obstructing but a lovely view—
But worthy: Contributing to the art—
I still could see, to my delight, The snow white blanket;
knee-deep it seemed,
Had filled quite up the space outside
The human vanished; in exchange:
A Magic Witch's Garden Green.
The moon it shone: an eerie light
That glowed like Halloween—
I sighed: both fear and delight
Did seize my soul— I hated this

And yet did pray, to the Lord for
Snow some more; so that in the
Morning's brave and honest light,
I'd know for truth what passed tonight
Was real and not a dream to set
Things right or wrong— whoever
Knew— the truth and false of what
Goes round and round!!
The Night must pass as we all
Know, and Morning's light with gratitude
Returns again with big delights
Confirming what the Night just
Glimpsed. This day was no exception
And the snow with all its nightly charms
Was there without some truant claims—
My soul did gasp— my eyes were
Hurt at such a dazz'ling sight—
Who cares for beauties of the
Seas or divinity of the high
Heavens— when the Earth, Abundant, can such a wonder be!!
The snows were deep with elfin
Charm— it hurt my spirit so,
To look upon such purity— i dare not sink
Or tread inside with mucky human feet.
— My heart then lingered, looked
Around for other things that might be there
I espied right truly, lovely colours: more or less;

The same from yesteryears or so,
Strong, true-green leaves encasing:
The yellow, nodding daffodils!

34. The Poi Delivery Man

The blowing of the
Hollow rubber-plastic,
Spherical, soft old textured horn
Sounds merry at the slightest touch
Reaches my ears like music of
The candy man or toy shop on
A bicycle.
That reminds one of a past
That existed long ago..
But is very much alive in these
Wise old Streets of Siolim.
These horns are many not just one
That blow pop popping gallant Through, the native village
Without the frills or fancies of Urban commerce and disgrace.
Prices fair, no, understated in fact; Not raised at all
Even by fairest of degrees,
To match the abominable tags
Of Boutiques and coffee houses or shops
That offer herbal teas!!
The Poi man's a noble soul
You don't pay much: it's such a shame
To do this though. You bring them home — the breads I mean;

Just back from selling at your door;
Still warm and waiting to be eaten
With butter, cheese or none
At all.
I'm going to spoil the rates out here
Full determined, take my word:
And strike a balance between the two —
The Starbucks prices or any other
Cafe's or fancy teashops in the
Rainy, dense green streets of Goa— the place that sells the Poi buns!
They have the cheek to sell
The very buns that come your way
For double triple of the price
You'd pay to your dear Poi man!!
Let's all together raise the worth and prices of these breads,
And buns, so charmingly called by native folk,
Bangles— instead of Bagels
As, they explain: "Sir they have empty spaces round;
Holes like bangles and so the name befits them so!"
Repeated gestures change the scene,
Pay them more, each and every time you buy
And you know you've compensated
For the lack of deserved
Attention to the man
Who blows his horn; in the rain or in the sun,
Delivers free the freshest, nicest

Softest buns you've ever seen.
PS— one secret let me share
With you— the two horns that
You hear - first in the morning
Then the evening sure and right
The morning horn is for the fish
You real may buy at leisure…
It's in the early evening so
That the Poi man delivers so
His sweet plain buns.

35. Another View

Who has seen a woman so
Seated on a yellow stool
With trucks and lorries passing by
To leave behind a trail
Of smoky dust and grime;
The lady combing back her hair
Tying up intently the decent plait—tell me why she'd perched herself
On the cobbled edgy roadside
To carry out activities of pure and proper vanity
When easily she could have
Better done the plait, and sitting
Home inside.
Could be it's a parallel to
People sitting at the top
Languishing over hours of breakfast
Sipping coffee, lulling over
Mountain tops.
Someone takes out their combs
And runs it through their pretty hair
Just as such the lady does
On the tricky yellow stool

With landscape turned into life support
Of daily pleasures want of else;
The dust and grime and groan of wheels
Heavy with the overload; the
Right beginning of this day.

36. Litti

The vested, bathed and hair-combed lad all finished with a full day's
Labours done; by 8 o clock. With long the stretch of vacant time
Before e'en the day's begun;
Stands erect without a smile
Or expression of any kind.
Not ever eager to sell his well
Arrayed fantastic trays of roasted buns.
Low profile for well he knows
Or maybe not: instinctive knowledge
Just as such—the means the end together are only one.
Labour is its own reward
Krishna was the one who said:
Do your duties well- don't worry
Of the just rewards; as they take care
With just as many.
Just to add on another fact— I'm glad I bought some roasted buns
They're fresh and humble; healthy, fine
With some spiced up chickpeas stuffed inside.
Can't buy them wherever you go
It's typical of these humble humans—

They're made on roadsides in Bihar.
A seat belt that I always thought
Was stupid not to tie when inside a vehicle
Of whatever kind.
Whether in front or at the back
When travelling far and wide.
I always cribbed for lack of it
But when I had it there; did not use it
All along my travel on the deathly speedy
Endless smooth and, sternest highway.
A thought nudged at my mind:
If I'd have to lodge complaint
Against a friend I traveled with,
I'd instant find a cause for any
Future unexpected ill
But alone I dared along without
The tug of seatbelt through the miles.
Why was i reckless when I'm not.
I continue even now without the seat belt on
Trees and fields are rushing by
Like the train that good old
Walter de la Mare
Described as faster than witches, faster than fairies…
The lines went on without a pause
In keeping with the fire and speed
Of the maddened whistling train.
I think I'm a little mad in the taking

Of this journey
If at the end I'm still okay,
I really couldn't tell of why and when
I changed my mind about the
One staunchest of beliefs
That everyone young or old
Should travel distance far and wide
With the stripy, gagging, two-inch seatbelt on.

37. A Village

This village was neglected by
The owners of this awesome land
And when discovered treasures there
With open eyes in wide
Surprise, it was a little late
Mind you, to sow and reap
And gather fair enough the
Precious fare.
The cows that moo in yonder barn
The fishes left to swim along
In the murky green and mossy
Fullest, deepest yellow Pond.
Birds that chirp a busy hour or
Two; in the evening and early
Dawn— know no hurry to jump
Into the next phase of the growing day.
Lanes are real and lay alone
Save the barking dog at noon
Or some half clad children where
Simple things of playing ball
A broken bat to hit and run
To the farthest field that blows.

Lord how very blest the men
Women, children, cows and
Other creatures too; of having lived their
Lives within this untouched
Land of owners whose thoughts
Were forever in the city; foreign
Lands— ugly spaces; strangest Men; compromises everywhere.
Lonely lost and loveless journey
Into one futile
Forlorn town.

38. Unexpected

When in the streets of this
Quaint land, I mind my way
To understand the wavy jig-jag
Motion of the roads laid out for
Men to come and go..
I'm shocked to find that my free hand
Is in a doggie's mouth that licks
And frozen to the spot I am.
Survival laws and courage born makes me not
To scream, as I sure would on other days
But frisk along; the dog, poor
Thing, as known to many in the lane,
To have three legs and limp along—
Picked me out it seemed, for
Recognition as I just passed.
Maybe the fear had filtered through
And sharp as dogs are to these
Vibes, he carried on with a low
Growl that was impossible to
Figure out— in friendship or in madness;
Whichever was, It was a nightmare
Just as so — a person who never

Had her hand so close to the
Awesome Canine breed!!
When at night I told my sis
She listened with such fright for me—
Not for what the dog could do
But burst out loud, in rejection
Of my act of rescue: beckoning
A lone young lad to carry me on his motorbike
Back safely home from where I'd come, "Pray take me home,
God bless you for your kindness so.."
God was with me on that night
The rightful fellow brought me
Back— Clyde was his name,
Fair of face as well as soul.
My sister warned me evermore
To never never mount a bike
A stranger could be worse than
Any beast or spirit; fast
Become a crime it could, if
He'd sped past the house I lived
And took me to wherever else, who knows!
And harm me for some wealth
Or any other gain!
I thought of the three-legg'd creature
Drowsy in my bed— now forewarned of never walking
Down alone, or at least hold always,
A spiky, smooth, lean or thick-any kind of stick in hand.

I wondered why and how he
Knew, I was a stranger
Come along— I thought and
Thought and hit upon: a fact—
It could have been my clothing
Such as I'd worn— a bright block
Print of orange-red from distant
Sanganer— that with the fear In my sweat made the beast
Do what he had done;
And also very clear to him: I was a
Stranger to this land.

39. The Village: The Wrong Side

Walking through these fertile grounds
Great the gifts that must you
Greet at every nook and corner here
Every step you take you know
That the Lord is with you ever;
High and low; leading through powers
That are still unknown.
Come you rich or come you
Poor; there's not a soul without
Some cheer; there may be dangers
Lurking in the shadows though
It would perhaps be wrong to say
That only goodness is what reigns
Supreme; without the hazards
Of human interference with
That carefree space that the
Lord created.
Goodness knows what ills
There may thrive upon the brambles where
Roses earnestly do bloom

And look divine to man
And artist; poet, painter
Every child who looks upon with
Wondering eye to reconnect with the Great
Expanse, Divine.
Good and bad; fair and frenzied;
Seem to wander hand in hand
War and peace do strive together;
In the furrows of this Land.
Let's not question why and how
The struggle gets to carry on
Between the polars
Who knows how—
The Lord did plan the Earth and Sky
To be away from one another
Only to look always up
And down— loving, gazing at Each other.
A mystery then remains to be
Just a mystery if you feel
That in no case should it
Be outraged out of context
Or pulled out of its own
Hiding place: with the firm
Belief that nothing or not
Everything should see the
Harshest light of day.
When in return you are

Given more than you ever
Had expected; you are blessed
Forever more. Extend the kindness you've been shown
It's never meant to stop with you
Give back to Nature what you
Owe by blessing, helping, being, loving.

Of Human Interactions

Crossing Cultures

Not even the majestic peaks of the Himalayas may reign in solitude.

Nothing...repeat: nothing in this world stands alone.

Purity of race and culture is a beautiful confusion.

40. Awake

Hush, soft gentle creature from Bethlehem
The air around you is lighted; glowing, haloed
The hour is past all earthly cares
And yet right here at your grassy door,
There stands your Master with a small brass Pail
Of blended foods and nourishment.
If someone saw; if someone knew;
The famous Lawyer known around,
For grace and knowledge in the Courts—
A little wily, handicapped with worldly Lordly cares
And lies to dress or quicken Pace, to save a wrecked-up soul
From ruin—so what if it is another victim—he the sinner?
Payed for winning—he does it right.
A fair and worldly soul; so full of wisdom: only a few his
Earthly flaws; he ventured through the whole long day
To make amends for what was right and so to
Stand in humbleness for you, dear creature
Here he is—repentance is the mood tonight for
Having lisped a frightful lie in courts where Justice
Always was, thrown to the winds, whenever so
Whatever for, we all do know.
It is no hour to express delight—

Maybe it's simple gratitude that brought
Your Master's feet abroad, and dragged him out of bed.
Or true concern that, tonight you might
A needful hour of hunger meet—you've been
Poorly, so just in case, you might right keep and
Have, close at hand, the nourishment to make you well.
A haloed moment just appears—this needs no stately
Introductions. They come inside in plainest clothes
Nude and smooth and brown and bare.
Such a moment, lucky you, has visited your barn tonight..
You stand still at the sight of him who
Cares for you, and he in turn with fondness,
Rooted at the spot; with sunken eyes yet right aglow
In favour of this moment lost to Eternity.
Your gentle lowing can't be heard by human
Ears or heart—'tis far too gentle; far too mild
For people's greedy grasp.
But there he stands:
The Lord himself to treat you well into the night—
No force to eat or bring you down with anger or by
Sheer strength. The visit is a special one, for
Who wold venture so, in the dead of night?
With sleep afloat, he's weighed good down
By care and wear and tear; the bucket full—
Slips— gladdened by a loosened hold,
Few inches down; a careful, echoed clang;
So no-one who's not wakeful still,

Will ever get to know; the episode
Right happening now—
In the making, in the next;
In yonder full Eternity.
It's been a while since Time stood still;
Two breathings mingled so, in the fragrance of the breeze
Outside; the warm and soothing, hay-borne air of Hearty, grassy shed—
Gentle brimming eyes that knows
No other pair of earnest brown—
The Godliness quick, the Hindus saw
In the love Supreme…
The frozen, chilly stars above
Spread out in inky, happy sky..
The magic trapped inside our
Minds: today, tomorrow and the next.
Immortalised in lines
As these in sprinkled Words
Made possible through memory ..
Vibes: A tale that's told;
Of love and bonding
Ever after so: Man and Beast:
One for the other does exist
God's complement to each alone.

41. I Want You To Know: My Daughter

I'll still love you even so if I ever come to know
That you can't care for what I say
Because of habit to carry on
And while your time away for something
That you're too used to doing;
Deprived the will to leave behind
The last thing you should have sorted For.
Gentle is the hand that rocks
The cradle so… but firm and cruel
Also is if danger threatens to abide.
A mother never leaves alone
The baby in the cradle so.
What a pity things should fall
Apart: for things that are just much beneath
The human spirit and this precious
Life in exchange of others;
That's more than just a place
And things we've fastened to ourselves
As more precious than our beings
Or our loved ones.

I pray and pray for lightness of
Your mind and heart and will
Continue just like this but I do
Pray as hard for me, myself: so
I may not stagger to miss out
On seeing you blessed and triumphant
In the chosen path that you have
Picked above all else.
I wish I could be more inspiring
Further strong; I hate to see you
Doing things without the holding of
My hand. I've waited quite along in Time
And now feel tired in the game
Of standing still— what did I do that
Things went wrong—for you and me
And everyone!!
I say this not to false support
My woes or money spent—
I only wish that I was spending more
On something that was better
For my darling daughter who
Has minded herself alone for much
Too long— let me hold you by the hand
To show you now that righteous
Way. Don't expect to do alone better than your
Mother being there with you.
Something surely is amiss; I

Cannot put my finger on. A
Just reason that sounds convinced:
To tell you that the last stretch
Should be taken with your mother
Walking alongside with you.
If you are proud —of my being there;
Show it with some love and care
For now too long have I stood
Alone, lurking in the shady Desperate,
Corners of our lives; waiting
Waiting evermore for the moment that with tears;
You will call me anytime from my hiding place; make me glad
and join me in my lone endeavours!!
I long for sweetness of your breath
Your fragrant hair, your fairy-tale
Person and Attire;
Flowers invisible; encircling
Your dainty, loving, stupid Cupid head.
The air around you fluttering,
Coloured, see-through, glassy, rare…
And whooshes of a raptured
Time that merges into everything—
Eternity?!
Keep me, Hold me
Hug me tight
I'll always love you
With all my might!!

42. Home-Leaving

Home is often more than not,
The place one grew up in; not complete,
Like an earthen pot to form; wet and glad to build up so
In their precious parents' hands.
The heat of summer's nearly over
It's raining hard only for an hour or two. Lovely
Gusty gutsy weather— my friend in need almost forever
But this special time of year
The rains sign up for the solemn moment,
It's leaving time: we'd arrived eight
Weeks ago, summer holidays—
Much awaited every year
Countdown has begun: each day as precious as no other
Lived and lived over again—in each moment
Limiting the waves of rushing Time in any manner—
Witchcraft is required—it's there as ever in desperate times
Like these of leaving home …
The eighth week's here,
It does arrive; as just as ever—no apologies—
All had informed that Time and Tide wait for….
No man.
Was ever a day as sad as this—one day before the

Noted date— tomorrow whistling,
The cheerful reddest train in miles around
Rushing through the small, untidy, though potential,
Eternal little town: at where my dearest parents lived.
Summer wasn't really short—a good eight weeks
To see it all—lazy, sleepy, funny, with loads of fun
All huddled up and bask forever in the goodness of
Sun and home; rain and thunder; endless cups and
Cups of tea—the finest in the land; brought out in
Little wooden boxes, every time to wonder…how lovely
Is the brew, the find; told by history, founded by the great
Conqueror, Alexander!
The day did pass like many a one; The rain sets in,
In earnest now. It's 4AM..
Whispers in the shadows of the early morning
Dawn; A distant sharp whistle Enters, piercing the Domain,
It speeds up: followed by many others—one can hear a distant
Chug of trains—one will take us far away!
The clock keeps ticking on and on…
It never sounded so very strong—
The freshest brew of Darjeeling
Tea comes wafting through;
All set; bread and butter—tea and tears
Secret from the crowded gaze—it seems that many pairs of eyes
Are intent on what to do, to make a perfect going-away.
The journey's long, careful planning went along, the last one week

To make it good for mother and for child..
Courage now, I tell myself
Let go of this, the merry crowd;
The garage door rolled up resounding: marking
A departure, screeching groaning in yet so many voices;
Lack of care or oiling of its hinges—Grown old with passing
slender, sly, and Sneaky Time;
My heart should have missed many beats
By now— the marking of my leaving… I'm young and
Strong and haven't noticed the extra poundings of my heart.
I wrap my Pallu round my shoulders—I hate the soot
And grime we'd face—the little darlings are still asleep
Except the eldest who says goodbye—
Anxious soul for everyone, She's worried that the milk
Kept long, would curdle in the feeding bottle—
I look down upon the joyous bundle,
Questioning a thoughtful while;
Twenty months— old enough to know we're leaving
Hugging e'er so tightly, me and him—
I think along…
…. The baby's mine; Thank God for that!
Everything that's worth,
Its weight in gold,
Happens on a rainy day:
The sun bakes dry the goodness formed,
And turns it to a thing that
Stays— for as long as it may

Stand— outgrows, outlives so
Many other things around
They say that houses when so built,
In the Rain, followed by the scorching sun
Are strongest with the alternate
Energies of each one!
The Sun; the dominating powerful One
Does find always a way
To creep, back into our lives
Again, again. It's the rain we
Waited for always in labour
Of the love..to keep us sane and wholesome:
The wet forming,
Holding shape and size,
Turning the clay laid out for miles
Into all that's wondrous and benign.

43. My Wished For Home

Unique is how I'd sum it up—
An Antique shop much like the Ramms' of yore who'd placed a thousand
Little pieces struggling with a
Little child who grinned as if it
Knew already the business of
Antiques.
Breathless, nervous always
Was the trip inside the antique shop
It seemed to match my friend's
Fineness; thoughtful, kindly heart.
Equally, it so did match the dignity
And handsomeness of her father,
Mr Ramm.
The place was crowded; far too many—
Dainty porcelain of Queen Victoria's
Reign; romance and beauty
Lived together in the figures
Small or medium; white blanc, blue, pink
Or sober grey…
Pretty, precious, lovely figures
That seemed to chime, so gently, as within

Themselves.
A tinkle of an antique bell
Which ushered in for welcoming
But only to a few who would truly
Buy some piece or two—
The door ajar, it shouldn't be:
The breeze was gentle though
Rough for these, little creatures
Breathing air, or so it seemed.
Anemones; vases, framed and
Smiling, stranger still, the faces
Of more than a hundred years ago,
Who looked at you wherever you went
A rather spooky thing you know.
It was a privilege seldom given
To others— I was special in every way
A dear friend of Caroline's and
Brown and tidy, come from Ever so many, miles and miles And miles away!
Maybe they thought, maybe they sought
Some antique vibes of an antique race
The oldest country by far approved
By this the world and so I stood
As someone who confirmed the place.

44. Let Things Be

Put Down the Phone
Some things are better left
Alone; unsaid. In a world that
Knows, no control of what to
Leave and what to take; of
Information, or of other—
Unbound, unleashed are the
Mysteries grand— that were oh! So romantic—
Life spread before us to unfold the magic gradual, patiently.
Today we stand in good control:
We have the awful awesome
Tools to decipher, to translate
Transform, the little, big of all
We knew and un-discover all
The wrongs and rights to great
Advantage: or maybe that's only what
We'd like to think.
A Kingdom gained
Is almost always—another Kingdom, somewhere
Else, unknowingly; lost.
On this let's take the time and effort
To undo some pleasures that we are

Now so used to—Lock the cameras
Phones, at once and use your eyes
To see the very real. Your
Mind is tired without you know-
Ing so… look hard around for faces
Where the earnestness shines
Through. We've all now missed
For long enough— twenty years
Or maybe more, when first I saw
The small device in someone else's
Hand, whispering words to someone
Dear— I froze in awe of what
It was…the smallest phone
I'd ever known.
Today I dwell inside my mind
Of yesteryears
Without the constant lack-attack
Of privacy that we hold so dear
And how it was delightful so to
Meet or greet a friend (or foe!)
Sans the forwards fast, sick and
Slick, with corresponding auditory
Blings and sounds to let us know
That people from around the world; not forefront
In your hearts always ,
Have wished you
For a bright new day— or forwarded now yet again,

A grandly spoken story with
Images abound: tempting
You to spend more time…
It takes just a fleeting second— So you may ready say: believe
Me this is so untrue— it costs
You every time you note: your
Inner vision; drains your might
Into these webs of man-made
Territories of virtual space
And that precious tick-tocking
Of the clock upon the wall.
We all do know in our deep heart's core
Wakeful or inside the slumbers
Of our selves: We've ended up Deprived of truth and loveliness:
We've thrown away some diamonds rare
For an uneasy handful of…
When again we looked upon,
Are gritty smithereens of worthless
Rocks and dirt in greed, returned.
Nature is the mother stern:
In exchange of rubies rare
First gifted with; out of love and care
From the mighty Lord—
Recreating Heaven on earth…
We're left in sorrow, heads hung low;
Impoverished we find ourselves!
To lonely stand

Upon the barren ground of
Our own, false-created loveless world.

45. Two Fruits

An apple for the sweetest, slightly
Seedy, most divine; fresh and green,
The guava held in high esteem
An awesome fruit all knobbly
Knuckles on the face
The humble fruit—give this to
Me, in exchange of the smooth
Bright red, shiny handsome apple—
I promise I sure will give, in right return.
My mother wouldn't know of
The swapping of the fruit.. the
Apple given each day, to keep
The doctor away.
Timed exactly so that the other
Had no grounds to cheat upon
Arms extended with timely pause
To give and take from one another —
The deed is done; successfully
Time stands still in history
An apple for a guava then will
Ever mark the joining and appreciation
Of: the humble firm and rugged

East with the smart and shiny
Surface of the West.
Deldom soes a hand that cares
Day or sare you for a sive
Into the sanderous ocean dining
In the dunshine light of eventide—
Son't go beyond the dhore

46. Lovely Sharon

We walked together
Sharon & I. . . But only
Half the way
To school we went
When half the way, her father on one side
Mother on the next; And me afar or left
Behind to join in at the time—
They left for us to carry on
The rest of it together.
So, we walked together
Sharon and I
But gladly only half the way.
The grown-ups had no eyes for me
A brown and stupid child indeed
Sulking all because they had no interest
And no glance or unexpected smile for me.
Sharon and I when on our own
Were happy as a pair of crows
With laughter on the long green mile
Still half to travel high and nigh—a skippety
Skippety hop and jump.
I do not know but I may guess, why we didn't

Walk back home, even if only half the way.
She was a special child they said,
With parents very old—what that really meant,
I think I didn't know. Sharon wasn't there at all
With the bell ring close at four; she left early
And was allowed because she was a special child.
I missed Sharon, many months together—
Didn't think of it so very much—she was a special child!
If I think of it again, I'd say,
I didn't even walk ,half the way, with her to school because:
If you split the walk in two; to and fro as many do;
Half the first to go to school—and nought of walking back home
—that makes it quarter anyway!!
Much I knew that she was ill, I often missed her:
Heavy-hearted trudged along; I'm glad I understood one day
A breezy cloudy afternoon—where she'd gone,
And for how very very
Long.
I walked back home in emptiness, neither proud nor bold;
When the grown-ups appeared all sudden—without dear
Sharon by their side.
They hurried on and swooped so down to catch me like never
before
It was like the meeting of three ghosts on a strange, ghostly
terrain.
Very soon we were back again on the pavement grey—into the
human world

Where honks of cars and barking dogs swiftly caught up with the day.
The grown-ups then with much sobbing, told the story out:
"Our Sharon's gone, dear Angel Brown;
She loved you dearly all the time—with
Repeated mention of your name she took
You with her soul along! God bless your soul
Dear Angel Brown—you are to us from Heaven sent—
If we could call you, love you still; we'd have you
Over live with us whenever time; however long."
I smiled for them and cried for Sharon, lovely as she was;
They followed me up to my house and at the gate they stayed:
With parting words once more:
"We'll come again our dearest
One: we've seen now where you live—for Sharon would have wanted us
To know that she still lived… In you so different from her though
You're even lovelier than she is…"
With this they pecked me harder still, on my cheek so lovingly
I thought of days I'd wanted them to do the same that they did now.
Damp and slurry kisses; tears mingled with their voices; fragrant breath…
I kept the moment in my heart and thought of Sharon there
Smiling happily e'er to see
Us huddled all together; Where the grass grew round
Our feet —And close enough the Primrose Hillock

Merrily nodding to the sound…
The world was still as ever; this moment captured fast in time
The parents' gone, trailing: far across the unknown pathway of
All time—gone and never seen again!
In my heart I'll carry forth the threesome
Always right beside, a merry walk or
Summer's stroll or in the dead of winter too,
I'll think of Sharon with her boots and mine
Sounding through the dense cool air, Digging
Hard into the fresh crisp snow and ice—marching ever
Onto school…even if it's half the way.

47. Mee's Summer Dress

'Twas the heat of glorious summer
Mother knew her daughter well
Having grown this size as
Somewhat big as any other
Teenage girl who was born and bred
In high and mighty Isle of England;
Had to have a summer dress.
Not too special would it be
As summer anyhow sparks
Up, joyful colours to extend a
Halo round to every tree
Or any living, breathing
Entity.
On shopping, looking here and there
Always for the very best Ma did spy and so did Mee :
Behold!
A gorgeous dress of oranges
And lemons with a splash of freshest green.
Small sleeves; round neck and
Ruffles too — and the child was good to
Go— Merry as a Bee in labour
Soaking up the sunny day;

She and Nature one and free.
Smiles and loving glances too
Floated gentle in the breeze
Mother compromised with just a one with healing powers of
Her own.
Everything does have a line
And leaves you wondering why
On earth should pure and total
Bliss be thwarted lest it cleverly escapes
The ruin of green and jealous Fate.
Mee rushed past a narrow way
Between the chair and sideboard carved;
When in one funny, irksome moment
The dress got caught onto the
Famous sideboard handle—
Ripped away a part left hanging
Like a meanful hand had torn!
Lord behold the grief that struck
The brown and pretty Indian
Girl!! Nothing ever could replace
Such deep regret—the brand new torn off
Summer Dress. Nothing new and nothing
Else could undo the state now that it was gone forever!
"Mrs Titmas will sew it up; "beamed mother with her cackle
smile!!
"Grieve not you funny little girl
This dress does not deserve your

Pearly tears— they're too precious anyway
Keep them for a rainy day— God forbid, that day should come
But to life's sorrows we all succumb;
Less or more is what we as
Mortals all do share!"
No respite these words would bring
Sewing up the dress was worse— the stitches spoilt and always seen;
The grief would worsen,
Mee was sure—every day a memory!!
The sobbing grew the howls
Arose when in the bathtub little
Mee splashed painfully the waters
Full— when washed and clean
She was amazed that she felt
Lighter: all her sorrows went
Down; when unplugged, the water
Drained.....!!!!!
Lesson learnt, dear Mimi now
All bathed and hushed as if baptised,
Was brave with tinkling
Laughter..run away into
The hours that remained

48. Gravity

I wait and wait for gravity
To change its laws; just for once
If not forever; so that we could float around
In good and awful weather.
No vehicle or company
Required for floating on and on
The act of floating would survive
Right on its Own— in peace without the traffic
Of hooting cars or human beings.
Laws would change accordingly
Keep guessing but create they
Will, another space another time
For changing such a changeless world
Into something after all.

49. A Family Saga

The sun has set
The doors are closed
The world is quiet
Inside their homes.
It's Friday evening
The shops are with their
Shutters down—
But running still
Are theatres to which
The family goes
To see a movie always
With a U for universal.
Early dinner; fragrant flowers
Pretty dresses, starlit eyes
Warmth and love from every side.
Baby dopey in the pram;
The five-year old awake
And keen to catch up with
Just everyone—not a minute
To be lost—you never knew what came up
Next.
Not to forget the struggling queen

The twelve-year old with bumpy
Ways and unsure steps—wondering
Ever to do what next.
The warmth and glow
And muddled love of child
And also man and wife;
With added charm of teenage vibes
Just entering into their lives;
How special this the evening then
With washed and scented bodies, souls
All huddled up inside a car,
A moment hushed up with a magic
So very rare—that if rolled up into
A bottled perfume one could buy—
It would be then a fortune spent
To have one, keep one and retire
To the magic extraordinaire.

50. Inside the Theatre

The theatre was not full at all
Some twosome threesome at
The most together spread across
Great gaps and voices that would echo
Even when they were so low—
They all hugged—the five year old
With grown up sis, who loved her best
The three together warm and happy
Looked upon the silver screen and let
Their minds to drift and swim across
The children's story so—Bambi the deer
It's mother too prancing to the tunes
Of the forest green and wild with spangled
Stars up in the sky and the glittery awesome moon
Light and shadows all night through
And then the casting at the end—
Was it really time to go—so short a
Break; how they all wished it could just carry on!

The Rain

Ganga was sunken, and the limp leaves

Waited for rain… The jungle

Crouched, humped in silence.

Then spoke the thunder.

- TS Eliot

51. Rain Again

I hope it's the rain and not the
Wash machine that's been washing
All day long. A waste of energy
I feel— throwing in a few stitched clothes
Not soiled really —just worn for only an hour or two
Corona's damages far exceed
So many others put together.
I look outside-to find the
Rain in a sober righteous mood
Willing to fulfil the earth's
And my own desires for it to
Carry on the Riot of nature
Healing well; without revenge
Or such respite— escaped from
Man's complete control…
Or not at all in fact to say
Man cannot conquer nature fair
He thinks he's harnessed energies
In windmills and in waterfalls
To turn the myth of Time and Space into bygone reality.
It isn't true— by far our race
Has never ever outwitted Grace

Of nature too immense and too
Bright for human eyes.
At the most it may be so that
Nature nurtures and takes care
Of everything and everyone
Who asks or does not ask at all.

52. A Mistake

The rain does pour with no control
The wet street shines outside
My clear glass shiny window
I am pained by my own heart
That doesn't beat, any stronger
Than before.
I am quiet at the change and want to say to my sad self,
That it's the place I do not own
Which makes me sad; not want to dance
With the peacock and the flowers
Nodding with the blackest Crows
Drenched in the glistening evening rain.
This feeling's new and hurtful too
I think it's born out of a grudge
I have against the Universe
For pushing me so hard repeatedly
To shake me out to a hundred different places
So that I'm left wondering— what or how or when to leave.
And everywhere it isn't all
The same: I have noticed to
My dismay that I have stopped
Wondering at the powers of

What it gives to us and why
It doesn't thrill just equally
In another place or clime.
Today the rain brings little
Joy, I do behold its advent
Though. I never in my
Wildest dreams would have ever thought
A moment when, the rain did
Fail to make me mad
With surge of joy and stir
Of mind or soul.
Today I'm disappointed with the lack
Of that familiar hearty happiness
Much before the rain had started
Pouring down ferociously.
I don't know how to accept
The dying of a constant friend
That lifted me out of depression
With just the sky having gone
Grey and the sounds of distant thunder
Rumbling through the angry skies.
It's not an easy thing for me
To shrug this new indifference off
It's like losing something precious
Or passing onto the Devil
My pure and honest only Soul.
I think again and I discover

It may just be a fleeting thing
And this detachment has come to me
Out of age and grace that welcomes
A dispassionate approach to
A modest realisation that nothing
Lasts forever.
But quickly to recover: as I'm not
Happy with the fact that I will lose forever
The pitter patter on my soul
Drenching me with love and
Care; renewing the world with
Freshness abound; to the rescue
Of the ground.
But that my dreams are always set
In rainy, cloudy days, it's true.
My most desirable happiness
Stems from dear Nature's greyest
Hues. What's happened to my
Soul's intent
To bask in everlasting light
That's not the sunny afternoons
But wet and precious drizzly
Streets.
As I write I'm glad that I
Have found an answer to my
Thoughts— I think I'm sore
About the fact that I have to wait

Patiently, for the rain to
Arrive and pour.
It's similar to when your best friend
Forgot your birthday or deliberately
Pretended to, so that when he
Bursts forth with loving and with
Party wishes; you stop yourself
From the urge to cry
With the realisation
That some things and people
Never Die.

53. 4 PM: On the Beach

Half-swaying Coconut trees
A distant haze and grumble
Shades of Grey White and Brown
The Sea in regular rumble of
Frothy edges pacing forth
Without a reason, without a rhyme
Unless exists a hidden secret, blind to our human eye,
The land and sea-scape just outlined
As Grey and Greyer turn the Skies
The grumbling blows, on— now backwards; unfurls
Exposes through Hindsight, the long deep buried
Vivid blurs of careful, stingy, somewhat possessed
Folded years, all stacked away, by one tireless Maid called Time—
Conquered though; disturbed, rude-awakened by Finite Memory…
Even Time would shy away from such beauteous Visage—
I think of School and cloudy Skies
Of Jamuns plump and humble-sweet
Staining everything on which, they fell.
Or lovely mouths, plump ruby-red, of all who savoured
A morsel of this God-like fruit.

Darkest Purple; Royal, fleshy, utter sweet—
In unison; something Raw—the scent
The flavour adding up to one hundred years
Of meditation, sacrifice of earthly pleasures, familiar chores.
Forlorn; distanced; hungry; Frozen and outworn,
The starving Hermit's endless cause—
With Jamuns that have infused our Beings,
And happiness of heart; the world's enhanced and
Going home, leaving friends and foes behind is wondrous
Good without the roughness of each day.. a calm descends
On everything.
Two flags are Red—put up by Men; The Sky is nude
The Sand and Sea lift up the Breeze
It's Time to leave; the weather's
Turned: strange— the far-off rumblings' now
Vast, fill up the vacant Air. The Sky;
A washed-out ominous Pink it is,
And not the healthy Crimson spread, our
Eyes are now so used to see…
Pink, bloodshot: The usual pretty colour, seems
Hideous, in this evening's scheme of things:
So misplaced, in dishonour of, the
Honest Red; keen to keep herself afoot; Afloat;
In an hour of Glory: the Rising and the Setting Sun. The Red
possessive, maybe she seems,
Jealous of her cousin, Pink—or could be a pure and
Natural longing for lost familiar: Hug of evening Sky;

The bouncy-angry Tide come in, in search of its friend, dear Red,
To join in eager too, our humble, greedy Human eyes…
Hidden sulkily is noble Nature's Red; not a glimpse or passive stay;
Not even in a dot —stern and glum the mood sincere:
Honest, clear, come what may!
Where and how are you today—Red, most drumming forth
And happ'ly marking off, each glorious, fast receding, tired day
We understand that you're Unhappy,
With the shifting pettiness—Rude;
The Pink, having so usurped, your Place—
No worries as you're a one Supreme
God-ordered rightful, Mistress of the evening Skies.

54. Sounds

Of the past mingle now with similar
Ones of this the present. It's a torture, to me at least;
To mingle tunes like these Tonight.
They're bound to as the Spirit grows, old but memories are just as young ;
Freshly plucked from the mind's
Green, rain-drenched garden; Bristling with dewy
Goodness; coming back to the soul in a gusty
Shower: of unmistakable apprehensions. Whispering with the
Warmest breath "No longer am I
There in body but to your Spirit
I belong and go with you
Wherever you do."
Further saying, "Honest true,
I hold you Dear: In the way that
You do Me."
My heart does beat with racy
Rhythm; overwhelmed with love
Of God and this: the God-Created Universe.
Superior
Everything that's worth,
Its weight in gold,

Happens on a rainy day:
The sun bakes dry the goodness formed,
And turns it to a thing that
Stays— for as long as it may
Stand— outgrows, outlives so
Many other things around
They say that houses when so built,
In the Rain, followed by the scorching sun
Are strongest with the alternate
Energies of each one!
The Sun; the dominating powerful One
Does find always a way
To creep, back into our lives
Again, again. It's the rain we
Waited for always in labour
Of the love..to keep us sane and wholesome:
The wet forming,
Holding shape and size,
Turning the clay laid out for miles
Into all that's wondrous and benign.

55. I Beg for Rain

It's surely not asking God for much
A pleasant rainy cloudy day to stay
Forever in the place I live or just to go
Away like a child who goes to school
And returns home so very very soon.
A lifetime spent in waiting, praying
For a change of weather
Although I love where I have
Lived in sun and wind and sand
I truly want to be there where
The skies are grey, the thunder rolls
The lightning strikes, the mind's
At rest, the body alive and prickling
To the cool damp air and not
Because of the sandy, mercilessly consuming heat.

56. Yearning

It's not a joke that I have lived
For years together in this land
Of heat and dust and little rain.
Complaints like these are out rejected
For the world's so ravaged
With more essential serious things.
To most the heat and dust and sand
Are the only truth of life but I have seen
The splendour of the green and cool
Of blue of sky and sea; of never
Giving up hope to look beyond and find
Treasures everyday in some corner
Of the woods or starfish on the
Pebbly beach.

Getting Married

Getting Married…

Is a holy bonding of two souls…

Exhilarating; Uplifting; Ultimate.

What happens later, is not up to you.

57. An Indian Wedding -1974

They're back now with the Virgin Bride
The group of men not women;
The custom is … the women
Wait.. at home with youthful lust and beauties
All tied up, to then unleash their
Passion only on their mens' return.
They're back and soon the air expands with
Anthems from inside the Mansion; decked
Up with flowers, fairy-lights; the drummers beat in ecstasy; the flutes
To soothe the spirits; wild with dreaming for so long—
And all the while the melodies, unparalleled in appeal—
The pervasive modest, gorgeous tunes of grandeur and nobility:
Shehnai Notes abound the air infused with rapture, close Divine;
It's indeed an epic grandeur, archetypal;
Growing stronger, with the passing of the hours
A ceremony that withstands the flow of time and
Unusual, jarring energies.
The Bride is meek but full of

Fire; the heat of day has burned
Her skin, though she's been wrapped
Inside the folds of gold and red
With a little bit of orange-green—
A secret; a mystery; no one's seen what
Throbs inside. Feminine limbs
Restless now with waiting for the
Final hour—of a union extraordinary…
Two balls of fire now rolled up
To be together….
It's been hours huddled
Up inside a car with the man she
Will be with now forever.
The sky's an airy purple, light enough
To see through the veil some twinkling stars;
It's almost like a water colour
Painting: wherein the crescent moon
Hangs on from nothing, jealous, undisturbed
In permanent territory,
Prominent and rightly shrewd.
The Bride sits in the middle of
The courtyard that's been duly washed and cleaned —
One after the other, women come and go;
Each time the special Aunt
She's the one important most of all—unveils the young Bride's
Mesmerising face.
The stars and moon do

Glad look down at every chance
They have. A bird's eye view
Is met to them delighted, awed
To witness this; gentle every time
The Bride to bare her perfect
Smile upon her Queenly face.
—A thick black band tied tight onto her slender
Wrist, helps ward off evil stares.
It's unique to see her crouch
Modest in a future calm: hard the ground
But never noticed by the Bride—
She has her own intensities.
Special Aunt most tirelessly,
With custom on her side,
Making sure that all should gaze,
Upon the Queen of Destiny.
The Bride showed courage,
Energised with eager waves That crash in-out; around her haloed being.
She loved the spot she sat upon— the holy ground;
Mistress now forever—
Of a pious-proud, caring stranger husband-lover.
The women with some children too,
Found it difficult to leave
To go away— the vision held them bound—
Her almond shaped eyes a-shut in mirth
With a smudge of earnest kohl

Each time the veil was turned away; but couldn't stop her
Mouth to play a mischief smile
When she was told to turn her face
Upto the stretched out coloured sky.
Who was last to see the rare and Elfin Bride ?
The handsome Prince who'd wed in haste
This dream-like virgin Nymph,
In full splendour and in throng.
A tall, lithe epitome of female
Grace and Charms; crowned with bright and glorious
Visage, — thin hoops; golden rings—
Three of them in fact; two dangling from two radiant ears,
And one upon the royal nose, were the only
Jewels that she'd kept on—the rest abandoned....
The red and golden layers of silk: thrown off!
In mercy of the sticky heat,
And now, a wisp of yellow, finest muslin cotton cloth
Long and winding though it was,
Showed her body like a Goddess; she moved slow and fast
together—
At once!
An awesome gait you've never known.
Women stared; not yet were jealous
And probably wouldn't dare to be—
Her tinkling voice and mirthful ease
Her stature and the love that showered
From the man who was allowed

To willingly possess; the Phantom Spirit who did steal
His heart and mind— captured
Here forever.
Life moved on like much before
The handsome couple rarely seen,
Hid behind the walls and doors.
The space that circled bold the lovers,
Became at once a watershed
Where Divinity together with Passion reigned; Well inside some
Ethereal
Bridal, see-through sheerest Veil.

58. A Brahmin Wedding

Holy fire; holy smoke
Infused within the mind
And soul. Modest, generous leafy branches
Spreading out like a Peepal tree—
A Nature-gifted canopy for chantings of the booming,
Asthma stricken Priest.
A bride without a face—Veiled: Wrapped in yellow—dash of red
Across her white and billowed chest
Huddled up for a moment.
Next—
To let loosen free, her anxious
Head of hair; shaking tinkling wrists;
Hurried chiming paint-pink feet And flowing, wispy yellow saree
In the wind that's not yet there.
The sun's not out- the clouds
Are gathered to look down upon
A place.
Archetypal.
Time did stop.
Captured hearts in smoke and colour
Muted sighs and eager sounds curling all

Around.
The bride now restless
Holding back energies of a
Different kind. A point in time
To change, embrace strong
Inflamed, dynamic throes
Of hidden, faultless, unknown And fleshly unkempt desires.
The smoke lies in the embers now
The cigarette air strangles, suffocates;
The clouds as witness have dispersed satisfied
Into yet, a peeping, eager, washed-blue sky.
The crimson of the sun emerges
Pale: Reflecting in the ancient dot and determined
Parting smear of utmost red.

59. After the Vows

A time ago.. a while ago
Let's think of what we were doing though…
Ceremonies now over with; Vows taken,
Yet not understood.
The awesome month of February—Just Married. Journeyed back.
A new home..not for him but sure for me.
A Queen, no less, dare one refer,
To enter through the tinsel town;
Open wide to proud receive,
The gates of love and passion true..
To be pampered; loved and all,
Bright and sparkling; sad and glad;
Both at much the very same; Onward moving melting Time,
Of mum and dad with sisters four,
Back home—that seemed so lost , forlorn, forgotten—
In some distant past that was,
Really only five days back.
One full minute was too long:
A daring touch, and there a glance;
Here a smile so meaningful, it seemed to say.
"We have a long long way to go;

Go slow—hurry not at all
To catch up with the dreary day!!—
A shove, a pull, a passing brush;
The breath as sweet as apple pies;
Oh what passion, what degree
Of oneness was this awesome thing—
A man I'd known for scarce some days,
Seemed like the only one,
Born that blessed hour for me!!
A honeymoon of sorts did follow
Away away to mountains fair
Mornings freezing in the sun— Bleeding…watery…barely there.
Me wrapped up, in meters five:
A silken sari, navy- blue; with shining borders
Broad; the silver threads so chafing rude,
Against my newly married, just-born skin—
Making it much colder
Still.
A black thick plait with weight pulled low
As if, right down—upto the shining, pebbly ground;
My thinking head, that firmly I, In a bid to rightly so,
Undo poor obvious Newton's Law;
Tucked deep into my earnest chin… my nose all
Shameful sniffing hidden; Black-wide eyes returning glares,
At nothing really, here nor there…
Fumbling for some words to share.

Words won't easy, smoothen out
Passions: overpowering as they are
Vibes of unknown kinds—
A furnace glowing deep within
And much to find before the air
Is crisp, mature, and come of age!
No boast of having done it well
It would take days to know and tell.
— Pure passion —
Has no reason to conclude…or
Commit itself to preset dues.
I stood there in the morning hue
Full ready to embrace: the new-found
Raptures of a life so unaware of petty strife…
A photograph was 'e'er so
Important, that you daren't
Forget.
The other half; the better half;
Erect in shirt and tie—all prepared to formally,
Invest the camera prim and proper:
Photos then were not so quick— it took a while to put together.
The job was done- an auto-set
Would muster up the gleeful trick
Of yester-year and worked it well
Were you alone or with a friend.
Wild passion frozen like the wind
Did halt while two most handsome

Men— myself and then
My other, better-half stood tall
And proud against the dark—
A shower of snow the trees did
Sputter onto our woollen, silk
Attire. So still we stood, a bit apart,
'Twas then the norm to not embrace
For the camera to do well.
So long ago was all this now—
So what? It's as if today it happened…
The fog embraced our slender, still —
Virgin bodies. Child-like innocence suspended
In the chill that held it there.
The sprawled out trees were conscious too
And black as black— the densest shades of morning wore:
And in the midst of holiness,
A sure crisp sound of metal made:
The shutter fell; the disc did whirr,
The photo shot forever—
Us locked into the photo frame
Today tomorrow, ever!!

60. A Journey

A wedding is a tinkly thing
To happen just once in a while
It takes a lifetime to assess
What goes wrong despite the love that you do share
For one another.
Create and ponder all along
Worth the while of hours spent
To make it go race and run
Through years and years of
Laboured toil.
You really couldn't guess
What when and how and why
You kept on just adjusting to
Passing of your time
And of others' too with the wish
That it would end
—The worry, not the tie.
However much it is said
That it is not the destination
But the splendid journey
That you've had
With one another— so true

Because the destination
Is that station where you're soon there
And sometimes is the final pause
I would prefer to say that stepping out
Together thus, when one journey ends
Another starts all over again.
Memories of fresh and youthful ways
Love romance and lustful days
Do impart the fragrance still
For you to savour and recall
You may walk another road:
One untravelled, wanting wear;
To seek, discover, other shrines
Of happiness and spend
The carefree hours that in your
Mind that you were always looking for.

Journeys are Forever

Journeys, literal or figurative; broaden the vision and expand the horizon.

61. Olive Green

I haven't seen such shades before
Of olive-green shimmering still in the
Grey and blue sober sky of this holy land.
It must have been there last year too
The shimmer and the green I mean.
But I haven't seen the colour then
What made me miss it I can't tell
Must have been my loneliness.
Trees of the same size but not shape
Modest: neither still nor wild
Just the right kinetic pace to
Instil inside the god-like feel
Of being whole once again.
Or never so to be honest ever
Such a calming numbness that infuses
Mind and body self and soul.
The green, the olive green will
Tremble within my heart for
Evermore. I think it's something
To do with my, little green olive coat
That Pa had bought from Harrods
Then back in the prime of life

Holding my small and sweaty hands
With the ice that had seeped through
My blue mittens with the lacy white.
They look cheap pa had said—
We'll buy you something that befits
Your beautiful brown face.
Pa told me later that the salesman
Who'd shown him the olive green
Mantle for his girl was amazed
When Pa expressed the need to know
If there was something better than
The olive green; suede and velvet
Light and dark; Coat that they
Then bought for lack of something
More expensive; more refined.
I marched onto the sleety, icy
London streets with the olive mantle
Hugging me— Pa said something
I didn't quite then understand—
The coat on you looks like a Queen's!!
That moment left us both spellbound
Not because of that he said but
In honour of the bond that God created
All along.

62. Lucy Gray

We all know who
She was and when
She took the road to walk away
On a grey and misty day
Never to come back again.
I look around to see and
Found that we have many Lucy Grays.. who've lost their way
To stumble, grieve: to never find their
Way to come back home again.
It needs little courage at this age
To venture out into the world
A good step taken is easy
Done but followed by a struggle to
Keep up the pace. Bittersweet the journey is
And seldom outgrows the mire
Only sinking deeper still
Every minute every hour but they grow sour, almost
Foul; for need of total attention
Of a selfless scrutiny
As what is best for humankind.
Working across the globe do many;
They take the pride in

Whatever they're doing
Earning much or earning less
It is a reasoning best to best;
To do exactly what the heart does tell—
Something other f
She went by air and
Not by sea; to build a
Future rare; where there
Were a hundred others
Just like her to take their
Share.
The climb was tough and
Unseen troubles lay ahead
At every step that further
Took her far away from safety and
The ground.
The climb did lose the way
Down again; it had to carry forward still
The sprightly maiden who had
Lost:All count of hours
Days and nights.
She had no choice but to
Continue still to move without
Delight.
All spirit lost— all future
Dreams a speck of ice and
Not anymore the dream of achieving those

Rare heights because—
What is high is rarefied and
Loses hue and texture both.
The goal achieved, how
Cunningly did Time pass by
No one really got to know
It's bad enough that climbing down
To start again is seldom given
To anyone.
With this as fact
Let's all rejoice with what
We have so that we may
Always do good to others
And ourselves too with
No regrets of climbing up
So far that we can't
Climb down.

63. Neuremburg

It was our plan for weeks on end
To go to Neuremburg one day and stay
There for the whole long day to shop
And wander free and daft expressionless,
As no one knew where you were from.
My daughter all of twenty one
Neither child nor teen, nor proper
Grown-up, deceived me into falsely
Promising to give up my only debit card
For all of only ten-twelve hours.
With the clock at striking Six
I would take it back again at the
Going of the gong— the biggest bell
You ever saw in the middle of the
Market Square.
Now it had also been a plan to take
Also the little grandchild too along
The day would just be beautiful
A mother of a pretty young girl
And grandma of a bubbly four or five
Still being pushed around
The pram an English one of navy blue!

I have to say that I am lucky
To have one prancing all around;
The other just to cuddle warm
Against my chest with the beatings of my own
And my little one's frisking too
Such orchestra divine it was— the beatings of
Both old and young—eager thudding pounding
Fast.
We hadn't entered rightly though
After departing from our town
We couldn't find the lift that would
Take us right into the market square.
No matter we were bound to only half
To understand the workings of the famous town.
Standing in the middle of yes, now in
The famous Markt Platz; we were all
Set to spend our time for shopping wisely
Free from doubt, and then at four to meet
The place where it was a coffee place or
The lovely Backerei.
Alone with grandchild
My heart glowed up— the first
Time since out at seven— unearthly
Time of wind and bower.
Baby sensed anxiety in grandma's
Deadly earnest face.
The poor dear knew it had better

Not demand or keep herself from
Oma's wrath of either money spent
On useless things or having not been able to
Return with equal funny lightness
Of a fun-filled day like this.
The elder left with right proportion
Of gay abandon and careful spending
But everything that she would buy
Would be something ever she couldn't
Have done without. The little one
Was satisfied with the promises that
Grandma made— one was that since Kaufhof
Had a better choice of decent toys— they'd
Better wait for when they were there.
Granny's eyes looked all around
But then there came a delighted sound
As if Anna could ever squaggle for
Something that was agreeable.
A doll or two did grandma buy
For little Anna to enjoy and then the two
Both agreed that they were hungry—
'Twas almost 2 by the clock.
Dear me, said granny, where's my
Silly, wandering daughter. She's so strong
In views: I bet she's taking very long
In judgment of what's good to buy—
She'd spend all time and energies

On this one day, taking it as the
Final race. Every trip an anxious one
Of thinking what to buy and wear.
When would she look around to see
The sunset, woods, rivers, trees?
Switzerland or Austria; New Delhi
Or old Calcutta, the pretty young thing
Always had the shops in mind at once—
The second thought might just well be
A pub-house where you could just unwind —
Murphy's Law was just the place to eat
And drink and spend a lazy afternoon
Free of cost because you know, Grandma always
Gave to Bui, her only personal debit card.
Li'l Anna knew that something always
Would go wrong if Bua spent too much
Time in and out of every shop. Granny
Hated every second of the time that was
Delayed in finding place to sit and eat
To make things worse, she was not seen.
Grandma tried a silly thing: she said aloud
Her daughter's name in front of every
Shop she thought, her daughter would
Attend. Looking out then quite afar
She saw her daughter walking fast with overloaded
Shopping bags!
The human Angel begged apology for being late

But granny with enormous heart and this time
Thank God she smiled, ushered into the only cafe that was in sight
The pram threatened to give way with grandma's
Angry rough and shoving ways.
It's not a story to get done so soon
It goes on and on way upto the moon
Meaning that the moon would be out
Before they would be back in their own town.
Luncheon done with struggle to enjoy the
Food as Granny said, the sandwich was an even
Lousier, replica of what they would make back home
In india on the iron grid with no real cheese to
Add along the uneven sliced cucumbers and
Tomatoes!!
Bah! She said, quite disgusted— even coffee served was cold!
Half the battle won, we moved along into the shops
With Bui. It did not agree with grandma all because
She was suffering on account of some thing
That made her run into the toilet off and on.
Kaufhof was the place to be as we could sit down in peace
And granny could go dashing into the toilet
Whenever this became a need.
Seated well at Khof now, granny was now good and
Kind— a box of ice cream chocolate squares
Were delightful to the touch, popped into one's mouth
A single block one at a time. But dear grandma

Was distressed, not so much that I, the little one
Was little and could bear the brunt of sitting still upon the bench
or sofa or the chair for these hours
Till Bui was exactly done with buying, in the process losing
Some belongings that she'd brought along.
Poor grandma always Bore the brunt of Bui losing
expensive stuff
Spending much and losing such was double agony for everyone.
One hour passed and then another; thankful
I was for just one other family of three from
Good old Japan. A child of three was good enough
To play with and to be; and Granny could go
Relieved to pee.
My honest Bui sure did come bearing
Shopping bags- a ton! Regretful smile across her face
And Grandma disheveled in such a state!
The return back home was dreary, sad as it was
Quite the end of the day; As if by magic I would say:
The part crimson, part grey; sky did burst into
A downpour of new delightful showers in
Pockets throughout the market square.
Just so to finish off the drama— a shabby coared
Gypsy-man, picked up his old guitar to sing
An olden folk song from England's Highlands.
Bui n me both looked up at Granny's face—
And she was smiling with the well-spent day.
With this then in her heart she sprung into

A trot— not angry with being ever so tired.
But I knew that some hurt remained inside her
Soft and kind but swelling heart.
Bui every now and then would ask her
If she'd rather spend another hour or so
Lounging inside some special place for
Dinner or for just a cup of coffee and some cake.
Granny was at her wits' end and stubbornly declined
I think she was maddened so; every now and then
To the toilet she'd have to run so we were all
Better off at Home.
Granny pushed the pram looking around at pretty
Neuremburg as if in farewell for a long time—
She'd had enough; however grand the beauty
Of the spires and towers of this famous land.
This wasn't at all the end of the day and
It wasn't about just catching the train
Back to hauptbahnhof, Erlangen, Alpha Hotel
Nice and warm;
With the train running steely, ever fast— we halted wrongly
At a station that was called none other than
Good old Feurth—
Good old Furth. There we stuck for hours and hours
Wondering ever what to do.
The starry night and full- moon sky
Combined with really cold and spiteful
Weather. Colder seats that were made warm

By sitting constant in one place; Bui and I
Embraced and hugged for the warmth of just
Each other.
Grandma put on a scowling face that hurt us
More than everything else. We prayed and prayed for hours
Together but no train passed by to where we'd go.
Cursing mumbling hissing spitting words and
Paragraphs each along, granny would have to
Loosen up for nothing known could ever be
Done.
All of a-sudden a train did halt— screechingly
To stop for hardly seconds ten or twenty
Scrambled on did we in haste leaving no doubts in
Our minds that we cared for ending up again
In an unknown different place. The station Feurth
Had had none else than the three of us—boredom is
A deadly state—it's better to be in some trouble and
To be awake.
Packets on the seat or tripping up each other.
Granny fumed and neighed and snorted
Showing no relief or forgiveness for the
Ones who were at home They hadn't really done
Any wrong but granny's heart and head
Both were on Fire!! To hell with all, she
Screamed; almost in the dead of night. Her voice
Dropped dead like a black cat in the dense, cold rich air.
Her son was shocked— he is my Father actually,

Granny gave into his remarks and explanation of what went wrong.
He said so plainly, matter of fact, would you all join me up,
My wife's been cooking mighty hard
To celebrate your coming back; sorry for the trouble taken but
It was your own idea to travel to Neuremberg all alone
With a gone-mad-for-shopping girl who twists you round her little finger—
I'm sure the little one behaved very decent....
The conversation lingered on till we arrived at Alpha's door—
Grandma rushed upstairs to the toilet—me, I jumped
Into my mother's arms but still was bothered with grandma's woes.
For the graceful story told, for warm food and
Some glasses of honest
Red and tinkly South of France, Geraldine Wine.
The closure was so heartening that it did seem
A victory over many circumstances. We'd learnt
Lessons— priceless; our day at Neuremburg!!

64. Crossing the Road

It wasn't really far to go
Maybe a typical mile or so,
Just like going to the baker's
Though 'twas longer than one thought.
Mother fearful of the fact
Crossing the road yet all alone
The child to venture out like that—
Every day to go to school.
Worried, desperate ever more
Ma was troubled all day long—
And then a humble soul did meet
And took the child in tender care
Like her Grandma on the wing.
The grey old creature who did promise
To cross the road holding the child
Would actually walk her all the way
Till she was safely into school.
If you wonder why she did take
This kind and stately act —
It's true that she was very glad to help a child
To cross the road
But also it was a hard fact that

She was poor and had to earn a
Pound and Penny on the side
To keep herself and cat alive.
The child skipped, jumped and marched ahead
Without real love, concern or care
For she who walked her every day
To good, grey, noble and serene
Jesmond Road, the very school
The child was every day to go
Skies were grey and she was true—
Right on time and never missed
Out on a single day— health or sickness; sunshine -rain.
The lonely woman, coat and scarf;
Grey- green umbrella too.
Marching forward soldier-like
Up and down the street.
Arrow-like the child would Dart, straight away
Into the interiors of the
Immense but charming Hall: where teacher welcomed Her with
crooked teeth all white but then indeed a lovely, honest,
Widest, brightest, ever the same,
Coral coloured Smile.
To cut a story very short
It happened so and only once
That Mrs Grey Coat— let's call her that,
Fell ill with fever in her bones
That creaked away in sympathy

So she no longer came to take
Across the road, the child who
Couldn't cross alone.
If absence makes the heart grow
Fonder: this was but a classic case—
The child would cry to have her back
The darling Grey Coat by her side.
If prayers sincere are answered
Thus: this brought the darling Mrs back
To the child's side as before
To run and skip and jump along
Again, in happy trippy road to school
(Jesmond Road to be exact)
With extra gratitude and mirth
Together they did strike the chord.
Of love eternal— old and new
Once more, in dreadful earnest.
The child did have the lesson learnt
What it is to lose a friend;
How much it matters when you have
Someone you can trust without
The need to worry or regret.

65. Balcomb Farm

The bus was taking us all
Together with our teachers two or
Three: To visit Balcomb Farm that is
From our school: 14 miles of wind and weather.
It rattled, bumped and drooled along
And gave us thrills e'en before
We'd reached the final destination.
The trip was meant to be a part
Of educating us with proper balance
Of country, town and city.
The place arrived and children
Tumbled out with glee—
Most of us had never seen
Or ever been to Balcomb or a
Similar place—a farm in the remotest Countryside.
The farm extended far and wide
The meadows were a huge expanse
The hurly burly farmers and
Their wives looked alike save
The heavy breasts and pouting mouths
Reddened from the berries eaten
Where and whenever found.

But people from a story-book
Another race of men and women
Taking pride in who they were,
What they did and why it was so.
They prided in the steady work
From the earliest hours of dawn
Till dusk did gather round the scene
To mark the closure of the day.
They took us round the farm with
Joy. The children went berserk
With joy to have today for only
Play without a single, mindful pause.
The wind the sun that mildly
Filtered through; to shine
On us was like a dreamy thing
Come true. The highlight of this
Day , though I thought would
Be the Barn where tens of cows
Mooed together in low sounds
— perfect matching of the place
Painted with an artist's hand.
They showed us how to milk the cows
And how they fed them and with What;
And all along I only looked
At their black and velvet eyes—
The cows' eyes where very little of the white
Could actually be seen.

It was a pity, honestly, to
Leave them lowing in the
Barn that smelt so good
With the creatures staying there
And of heavenly
Hallowed, yellow, hazy Hay.
No wonder Jesus chose a place,
To be born into the world in
A barn with the cattle lowing
Welcoming the baby King with
Such dignity and grace.
Further on into the fields
The farm was full of things to see
Big haystacks did prevent us from
Carrying on the tour and noting
Now and then the things that
We were told.
The winds did blow; the sun behind
The clouds did hide; the sky was grey
And then turned black with the
Passing of the day.
Some gusty showers— all did
Run inside the Farmhouse, warm and cold.
The kindly people gathered round
To serve us some delicious fare
To see that we were doing well
In their native air.

Very soon and it was time to
Go back on the bus to town
To school at first and then back
Home—
As usual on the rumbly road
Everyone but me did sing
A song wherein my name appeared
Somewhat in fun this song was sung
At my expense but was no real crime—over time
I'd learnt to take this in my stride
No tears threatening to roll down
My grubby, reddened cheeks
From the long day spent in the
Mild but piercing Sun.
Very soon, washed and scrubbed
Changed and happy with the glow
With warm, familiar food and
Din, of the day come to a glorious end
I snuggled into bed like every night,
Only that I would have the thoughts and hear the heartbeats
Of the creatures in the Barn
And see their velvet gazing
Eyes, forever in the dark.
Christmas means just not to me
A single lonely day; a festival— the magic of
Which will go away with the finish of the day.
Of a bygone time stays forever

In my heart and thrills my
Soul like nothing else.
I hate to have a headful of
Some issues that have to be
Considered or resolved.
It's better to witness other's stories,
Fun and woes;
Actions so as to enjoy
Them all on fuzzy celluloid.
This brings along with thrill
And cheer and along with it a mimic fear
A ceaseless flow of highs and lows
From which we may choose to either stay or better still—
Whenever you want to wilfully,
Break the tensions;
Arise and go.

Contemporary & Documentary

In the evolution of all human society, there are trends in fashion, food and sentiments... These are important for they are, what Eliot says, the objective correlatives of our wonderful complete psyches.

66. Amul Butter

The village lad wondered thorough; at the sight of hidden gold—
Why a slab of butter wasn't
Meant for him.
He wondered more because it was
Locked inside a cupboard.
Stranger still, he sure did see
The butter with a wrapped up
Cover drowned inside a little
Tiny tub of water right in the middle.
The locked up cupboard stayed that way
Till It was time to serve
breakfast
To someone who was special.
Mad he was to ask an angry looking woman. An explanation
For the butter—
Shouting all the while; revealed the
Secret, "You stupid crow so do you know, without a fridge to
Keep this in; it would melt into
Nothing; lose its flavour; shape
And size. Drowning the precious golden slab would retain the
texture, taste and shape."
But screaming at the wondering Lad for ever daring

To want to know and ask,
The last retort felt like a slap—
"It's not for cheeky lads like
You to stare and wonder at!"

67. Bread

Was white with light brown
Edges- the middle all so soft and woolly;
Very Light. Some people liked to
Keep the entire airy light as a feather
Loaf unto themselves!
The bread combined with
Golden butter brought back
To life the tired soul. It was
As if a dying man could breathe
Again and sit upright just in
Time to dodge the show; the Hearse
And be transformed to someone
Of another kind.

68. Lifebuoy

Lifebuoy was a soap to many
Many people. If for bathing,
They kept it whole; while if it worked to clean
Only the hands after the toilet dues,
It was broken as and when required
To be so diligently used. A bit of soap
Meant clearly that it was for
The dirty job—
A whole one meant sure enough
That you could freely use it up
For your long and leisurely bath!!
Some people were averse to
The pink- red bar of soap
And didn't want it either in their bathrooms
Or on the basin widely used just
After you may really need to wash your
Dirty Hands!!

69. Liril

The launch of Liril in our lives
Beat the poor lifebuoy soap
Out from constant use. The Liril bar created now,
Determined by clever science masters
Was meant to sweep clean its
Poor but useful Predecessor.
Liril sounds so very fresh; it
Was a pretty name that invaded
And set fire to the minds of
Generation Next.
The inside of the wrapped up
Soap was true unto its name
It burst with colour and a fragrance
That conquered time and space—
A heady combination of earthy
Limes and lemons; with some
Note of heavenly incense not
Obvious to many.
It's strange what magic is infused
With the colour of spring green
An oval contoured shape with
Lime n lemony fragrance bursting

And surrounding the very air
Around we breathe.
Let's not forget the pretty Babe
All of seventeen, who dived into the
Fountain springs for advertising of the
Soap, Liril. This hit the nail and
Paved the way for instant
Recognition of liveliness that would
Accompany the fresh green
Oval, textured soap.
Sweet Carol, also served the Nation
In many other ways— a leap it was into a
Space that brought along
Much to mark off new beginnings
And also equally to end many
Miseries unspoken.
The red-pink soap did thrive—
It was meant to remain that way
As many people saw the Liril price— two rupees and fifty paisa—
As very very grand.
Lifebuoy was the modest constant; affordable indeed:
It's democratic shape, size and
Smell appealed to big and small
It stayed and stayed until forever
In that tiny corner space for duly washing hands.
Liril was the next in line to stay

Not less than forever. It was though
In a certain way only second to the first.
As many times it is true in such the case
That the second, maybe better
Cannot outcast the worth of
Its long-established predecessor.
The story ends right here, and we still find the two of them
In constant if in backbench State.
The market's flooded with
Exotic soaps that reach beyond imagined
Concepts; combinations: heady
Clear, this and that— purple Blue green and pink; Brown and
gritty smooth and crumbly—Thankfully they still have not
Invented yet one that is black Fragrances too in abundance
Have lost count of fretting combinations.
The soapy world goes on and on with
Strange and rapturous known- unknown heady combinations.
However, then the history of
The soaps here mentioned
Rise; there's no mistaking of the fact
That they are the Founders
Of a race that's made the Nation
Happy, clean. Not anymore deprived
Of lasting freshness or of
Happiness and good moods.
This surely is beneficial for the Budding of the Nation.

70. Halo Shampoo

Another prized possession of
The individual who was struggling
Within the family then, was the two or three
Shampoo bottles one at least
That should belong inside indeed
Every girl's' impersonal cupboard.
However, all could not afford
The single bottle bought— it then was
The earnest duty of the one who
Had it all— to share with decency
The liquid to be brought duly back
Again with just a little gone.
A mental mark the owner would
Remember just about, how much was needed (not out of stringiness or spite)
Of the liquid only to clean well
And set right.
Long hair has always been
Admired , without a doubt
I say, but lack of goodness in
The cleaning makes a thing of
Beauty not worth caring for.

And all you do to pamper it is
Oil it heavy, dirty scalp and pull
And weave it into a tight and thickened plait.
No wonder then that Aunts would
Secretly get their nieces' hair
Cut short, one sleepy afternoon, from the angry mothers
Who couldn't reverse the fact.
It's nice to think that sisters
Could do that sort of thing
Back then, nowadays it would
Have meant a violation of a
Norm, not accepted, not at all.
To return to our main thing
(This to return to in a later conversation)
Let's think of the biggest bottle
Ever to invade the shops calling
Itself the name: Halo and later,
Halo Egg. It was the rave; it
Was the rant of happiness for all
Who had long tresses for to
Flaunt and care— put the nightmare to a
Gloomy end. Such cleaning fluids
Would enhance the beauty
And surely too remove the
Lice that threatened always to stubbornly be there.
The yellow brightness of the
Bottle and the viscous mass inside

Smelling lovely every time
The lid flew off by the owners'
Intended nimble Hands.
The substance promised not only to
Cure all hair problems that one had—
The only lie that followed imagined
Truth, was it never on its own,
Was able to bring out the lice.
The lice would need patience
And indulgence of a loving
Aunt or grandma; mother couldn't
Handle the impatience of her child
Or take lightly, without scolding;
The lice that came not on its own but
From sharing pillows and filthy, dirty broken, substandard
Plasticky, illiterate red-blue shady Combs.
Nonetheless however grim it
Was to ponder and reflect how
Girls' hair did follow them and lead the way
Into the day. It was a treat when the
Lice were out with strong bold
Tightened wooden combs that
Could be pressured to change into
A row of clenched and useful
Teeth.
The lice so neatly, nearly gone, the lovely Halo
Yellow Egg would smoothen out each lovely black -brown strand

For new freedom that was attained
In such washing of the hair.
Sharing so extended to sober
Friendship, mutual trust and
Gratitude that would at least
Survive right until when the
Halo Egg between them, continued
To exist ; not empty but still filled.

71. Chelpark

Was the ink that stained the
Clothes, the books and walls
Alike. There were no known funnels
To pour it right, into the column of the fountain pens.
Ink back then was very special
We had no biros or any other
Way to write on paper save
Pencils but grown ups would
Feel embarrassed —
Pencils, chalk were meant for
Children, teachers, not for Youth or stately Men.
Chelpark used to be a prized Possession, owned by those who were,
Quite rich in every sense— More than just a surplus
Of wealth and money. In days
Of yore it was the thought that
Education was the King of almost every other thing.
Black and blue the only two
Colours first, and then black-blue
Became a favourite one for many
Users, one by one.
Discovery, for it must be born

To each and everyone, Especially when there's a need like this
To save us from the dreadful
Task of pouring out, however careful, cleverly;
The liquid ink from a wide-mouthed, squarish,
Ever-eager, ink-filled bottle of funny shape
The plastic dropper that appeared
Made life so much better: to run
Slowly, drop by drop; the lovely ink into the
Fountain Pen…
My mother then announced to us
And told us we could in similar way, do the job
Oh! Just as well, with another, better
Dropper, of finished liquid medicine —
For ears or nose or eyes:-a brown and small; dusky, smelly
Bottle from the corner Chemist.
The word did spread and so the pot
Had now a friend, the plastic wobbly or a sturdy nose-ear
dropper—
It wouldn't spill, It wouldn't stain the hands or shirt of white; or
thank goodness!
Neither—The rather gritty, window sill—
The favourite spot to carry out
Such a special, careful job!
A prized possession still it was
For many many years to come
It gave us lust to carry on with
Boring and for mundane work.

Thanks to Chelpark we grew wise
In knowing how to reproduce
Things we learnt and then
became: Very very clever.
Very soon or so it seemed, ball
Pens did replace the dark mysterious
Inkpot that had stood the test
Of time,
Was very much an inspired thing
A status symbol in the midst of
Latent or of obvious lack of
Many other things and sometimes poverty.
It was nice to think of Chelpark
After many gone by years—
It's brought back memories
That stand upright — the values
And the living norms of people
Who were free from excess of
Availability— knowledge, information
Of each and every kind. No one needs to
Rewrite these with paper and a pen.
But progress keeps us so replacing
Both Beautiful and Ugly things
Three cheers for Chelpark anyway,
The memory is there to stay.

72. A Compass Was

Rare and precious; something to be
Stolen, daringly when no one else was watching.
But no one did because it would be
Immediately missed.
Public property, labelled well; perched exactly
At one place for all to use,
And then put back earnestly
Without misuse or mind you,
dropping, or any other known
Unknown, intended unintended
Injury to the half-alive entity
On the concrete floor.
The compass was a coveted
Thing; the pride of science,
Laboratories — spreading
Wide its four hands in reaching
Out to many peoples, cultures of the world.
A tiny thing, a piece of joy
Brought forth to navigate and
Find, discover treasures, countries,
Unknown to Man. Landmark discoveries; superstitions Gaining
ground with explanations abound.

Perfect round and black and heavy
Shining, fragile, much exciting— for the wonders it could show.
Amusing it is to recall
Never could anyone except a few
Know the reading on the dial.
Guessing was a thing considered
To be the truth; to each his own:
Directions of another are no one
Else's business— once again,
To each his own; the consequences he would
Gladly face and bear.
It's now a common easy thing to
Look up NEWS on your cell phone
The magic of the Dial is gone
And no person is confused
Over where or which direction He is standing at. No one asks
And no one pokes his nose at all
For right directions any more.
North, South, East, and West
Remain a Godly mystery.
Man attaches many things
To connect with all of these.
The guiding star that well determines
Your triumphs or your woes.
Not restricted any more for
Navigation on high seas
But something that will help

You finish all your blessed chores.
Rituals that are happy, solemn, grave
Birth or death or ceremony of
A different kind; we all need
These four forces, Angels of today
To carry us smoothly through
The rigours of the life we lead
Achievements of our wildest dreams.
Dreams that scare you; efforts
Nulled; thoughts and actions
All aligned— why does failure follow you; dog your steps,
Wherever you should go? When troubled or unhappy,
Depressed or unevenly sad,
Move around the other way
Try your luck and you might find
The answer to why you feel this way.
Directions will continue to
Rule the stars and Heavens
It's still something to reconsider
With the passing of each day —
For Vaastu or for others' sake;
To smartly follow rules established
By the Pandits wise; avoiding some lurking grim disaster
Or at least to minimise the
Twisted turn of Fate.
Something's of a main concern:
To help you ease your troubles—

That you may never ever go to bed,
With your restless sleepy head Pillowed in the North- the only
time you
Ever would, was when others
Laid you down.

73. Bimbo

BIMBO

Was not my personal weekly magazine
It was for my sister who was
Small
And bought in addition to my very personal two—
Diana; Tammy— all three arrived
With the morning heavy rattle of the
Never-or-only-hardly-seen, Newspaper, delivery man.
Every Saturday was expected
The arrival of the three—
Two for me and one for sis
Who was actually only three.
She couldn't read but she made out
A lot of things that we could not.
The sound of the three rolled perfectly;
Securely tied up with rubber bands— the kind
You'd never want to tie up
Into your long and lovely hair;
Along with the one that came
On a daily basis; the Daily Telegraph back then…
Pushed through the opening of the door to
Fill the caged box inside, made me jump

With uncontrolled and fierce glee.
Once inside the blankets layered
Alternately of blue and white;
I turned upon the sacred pages all too
Consciously to start the reading of
What thrilled me most— My Father; My Enemy
Was the one, followed up with Up-To-Date-Kate and Mysterious
Billy Blue; Ransom Red and Suffering Meg;
But best of all was always saved—Run Rabbit Run—
To read towards the very
End. Like you keep the ice lolly
To share with no-one but yourself.
Time did pass as it will do
I grew young and pretty too
Looking for some other things
To satisfy my natural human curiosities
And rising, fumbling, youthful cravings.
I turned to Jackie soon enough: a mag for
Teens and only understood
A few, of whatever it said or showed—
Tampons, rubber johnnies, gels and lotions as they were called;
Invaded the child-like gentle space
With many other things like those
It scared me to see how much
I would, have to know to turn into the distant
Woman whom I clearly did not know.
And so retreated safely then

Back to my thrill-filled Saturdays;
For Bimbo, Diana and the understated Tammy—
Which really was the best you know.
(This was a secret I did keep from the world— it was mean of
me I know; to keep this insight to myself). Anyhow,
Apart from this, my conscious
Action to Retreat, saved me from becoming
Young or old — (that's what you are when you're a Teen) at A
time it was not meant to be so.
I won't blame Jackie for all the
Scare—I kept a phial of
Perfume packed up in a textured
Thermal Bottle inside the Mag
For free; it smelled divine and
Stays with me in my youthful
Dreams today— the reigning
Queen of all Time. A hint of sadness too
Prevails like most things of the past do too.
And though I'm old and worn out too
Like the memory of the magazines,
I have the fragrance in my soul —Pity that I never knew the
name
Or else I would have had a
Chance to reconnect again to
That priceless phase of being
Both a woman and a child,
Drifting through a time and space.

Shh..Sacred

The page dare not hold all that's to be told…

But trying is no sin if you try with reverence.

74. Shh…

A sacred voice can sure be heard
Look out for this whenever you can
It may catch you—only sometimes, Unawares.
Voices of our Reverend ones
Departed from this constant
World, are blowing in an unknown breeze—
Stay still, they'll whisper in your ears.
They seek not—
Acknowledgement or any other earthly dues
From mortal men or other things that breathe
Creativity—away from Sun and Moon or such,
They lie in vacant space—special as they certain are.
They lie alone, our Reverend ones; transcending
Time, transcending Space—away from any
Beck and call; from claims of long-lost Ownership
Or Recognition in known form.
Give not a name to tie them down: Erase known facets
From your mind—keep an open mind and heart
Don't miss your only happy chance that your pure
Soul will sure attain: Behold their presence,
In this your unblessed state—keep patience:
They will touch and bless your way.

75. Footsteps

Yes, I can hear footsteps of a different
Kind. They shuffle when you least expect
They're silent when you don't
Neglect the fact that they are
Always there.
Shuffling here and shuffling there
At times when all the bees are humming
Or when yonder boy is
Strumming— his father's
Gold but old guitar.
Keen and silent are the sounds
Of our dear souls who made the trip to seek anew:
Who wandered once too far away ,
To ever reach a point from
Where they might return to
Where they had left behind
Their elemental even song.
Come stay with us you shuffling
Feet: we miss you much in your retreat
Come to stay and liven up
The deadpan of our awful state.
We promise not to interfere

With your notions, new attire;
With your dreams and
Aspirations that clearly give away
The fact that your needs are
Various—few or not is beside the point.
We lost, regretted; regretted lost;
Please help us to retrieve the
Loss for gain of wealth and health today
In your great and priceless
Presence; and mischief
To return for mirth and ease
On that everlasting note.
Whatever your cares, your loves, dislikes;
Our willing hearts do oft' aspire,
For your return in any form.
Give us back our hearts' desire with the
Grace of living life, in the midst of all you be
Warm and shadowed; green or brown—silver, gold or purple
Gown. Wrap us up in your embrace, in your
Presence, so Divine.

76. Home Again in Gaya

I am hiding away from you
In another part of town.
I feel your presence all around
And am ashamed of not
Knowing what to do and how
To answer to the newness of it all.
I tap the phone and all are there
And recognise me with your name
With reverence and with
Heartiness, are ever ready to
Extend a helping hand, no matter
How the years have flown.
I've always noticed that I've Never suffered in your Nest
However bare it shows itself
It is the place that knows no
Want or ever fails to soothe
The heart; wipe the tears and
Bring back again the joyful cheer
That's known to only those
Who've had the choicest love
Of you alone.
The winds that blow around

This blessed holy Land have
The essence and the fragrance
Of both my precious parents
Who, without a flinch of painful
Thought, reside forever in our
Hearts.
Always more than I would
Desire, dream or dreamily aspire.
As if in understanding
Of, for all I care and wish to
Have.
Blessings make me shrink
In size and my consciousness
Expands to dimensions hardly
Known to any man.
Thank you for this second chance
To lay my being next to yours
I do not know the turn of chance
And what really brought me here
To where I am living once
Again.
I think I know why this is so—
I came back here to see once more this
Lovely place so full of saintly
Souls who do reside within the
Walls of Divinity.
I come back now as old I am

Also to unite with me: myself: the child that
Still is tugging at her mother's busy
Apron strings.
Or once again to hear father's
Happy voice, full of stories; spooky, fun
Or to jump into the good old Fiat car — green and waiting for us all
To drive to Bodhgaya on one Not so busy Winter evening;
Humming, singing, giggling
Still, on our darkened journey back; the
Narrow single road with speaking rustling arching trees for company: The path that leads to
Home Sweet Home.
Wholesome thoughts with meals
To eat: the holy food so pure, it glows
From frying, spluttering, boiling
Scaring all bad things away
On the sacred fire.
Both exotic and simple fare—carefully cooked and sometimes when the mood was there
Savoury, extraordinary things.
Nature then did never fail
To surprise us and trip us up
With a distant rumbling of
Thunder unexpectedly;
Or in the middle of the night
To jump awake at the familiar screeching of

The Gate, with Father coming home
Very very late!!
With Ma shouting out aloud:
Tomorrow morn, she swore
She would, convince father to
Go to work much before the strike Of Noon.
This never happened
All was the same, till the very
End.
He would go at noon and back Returning at the strike of twelve
But come winter and it changed with the goodness of the
weather
Keeping people healthy and the doctors would not be
Called upon
Earthly or unearthly hours.
It was good to hear the garage
Gate: made of iron, rusty too
Screech by seven or eight o'clock
When everyone could see the moon hanging low and shining
bright
Still in the chill without a wink of sleep
In the ink blue dotty, starry
Velvet of the night.
There's plenty left to talk about
To think and laugh — be grateful for
But maybe to continue then
On another grateful day.

Please let's start to say just this
That the memories of the past
Are worth the madness of the soul
To reconnect and have retold.
I wish it had just stayed that way
Forever for whosoever cared
For change of place or people—
None!
Only to say once more that
I'm not ungrateful for the passing
Of Hooded Time that seldom
Shows, the smile, the tears
She does gracefully withhold.

77. A Reunion

Every time I pass this place
That my father lived in once
For thirty years without a pause
I stagger at the sight that gives
A missed one or two or more the
Beats that confuse me and my heart.
My head hurts and my feet do stand
Rooted to the wet and crunchy ground.
I look askance at the sky in
It's mighty blue spread out
As if it was a huge big thing or a creature
Shapeless but would never perish
On account of having such a rarefied
Affair with the elements around.
The ground has always been a
Friend of the sky and clouds that
Bear the brunt of changes here to there.
What is it that makes the world
Go round without reason, without
Sound of any clue to rapid circles
Hard to feel or hard to think.
Destiny and the facts of life

Our genes our will and situation
All go into building up our
Meagre and our strong attempts
To give this life some size and shape.
Destinations seek and strive
To find their owners far and wide
Or is it just indeed just this
That even so our destinations
Are only ones that are destined.
Be careful of whatever it is you
Wish, for Fate may easy misinterpret
And land you into dire trouble
Of a kind that never was imagined
Like when I prayed to the good Lord
To bring me back to this the town
Where I belong. It's good to have a second chance
To live and savour and correct
All that went completely wrong
In the past. The present has the
Better powers to extend a helping hand
And make sure of the fact that
Each one will have the chance
To make amendments good
And strong.
Don't be taken with surprise
If what you'd asked for did
Not rise to the heights you'd

Anticipated for the mystery
Lies behind any past or
Present Time.

78. Mum

My mother left for God knows
Where. We're not supposed to ever
Know so it's only fair.
They will return, you know for sure
But maybe not in the way we
Knew them to be back then
You may find them anywhere
Just look around
To see them there beckoning
Eager, kindly, utmost fair.
Go ahead to then embrace
Whoever is there to give
And take your love
In return- nothing more or nothing else.

79. Life

When dusk gathers like it does
It quickly fades into the night
That like vapours, descends on
Us.
It takes advantage of the dark
To make us sad and lonely where
The beatings of the heart do find
An awful echo all around.
Come but morn
The sadness dies
A natural and a peaceful death
What in this life if full of care
We have no time to stand and stare
The evening comes again today
To link up with the fleeting day
The not so fleeting darkened night
With all its vampires and delights
You know you're dead
When once you lose
The weaving of the day and night
Into a mono world of blank
Be it silver be it black..

We'll never know because
We can't come back to tell what was
After we are dead and gone.
It's good to feel that there is
Life after this one closes down
But painful is to let all go
When one has nurtured friends
And foes— lovers, brothers, girls
And boys together with those all around.
It's the faces of the ones
That you gave birth to
Long ago— to lose
Sight of or
Deny the painful parting fast or slow.
We don't choose the day we're born
To whom and when and where and why
We don't choose the paths
That offer myriad options
Of tomorrow.
Once we're done we're done
Forever and forever.

The Lighter Side

Mirth and humour are the two pillars of Man's well-being: look around and you will find lightness of heart everywhere.

80. The Happy Fall

It's sometimes good to trip and fall;
I see it as a comic pause
From the boredom and the floating
Of stupid old domestic chores.
Be still awhile and just make sure that
No bones are broken; head or limbs,
Scan your face while on the ground
The pause is valid and profound
For sympathies are abound, just as you go flying down.
So take good stock of what's gone wrong.
Before you stand— you're allowed to pass.
Once you're sure that you've been lucky
It's good again to quick discover
The joy of falling
Not too hard— stay longer on the cool floor
Enjoy the mimic disaster that does thrill
But safe from copied, potent dangers
To the tired mind and heart.
It's fun to know when you can gain,
Get up and clamber tall once more
In the focused victory; glamour of a small defeat
In the flying of the air

And limp back for your favourite chair.
You no worry you no care
If you hear some muffled laughter
It's in good faith and intent
Of missing the possible disaster—
Of breaking, hurting special parts
The trick thus lies in only this:
Allow yourself to sneak a smile
Better still, just laugh along.

81. Convent Elegance

The elegant nun went out for a walk
Without paying heed to bramble or ground
She was wearing black shoes
All pretty and polished
Her veil was a shining white
Clean and crisp in the sun.
Nose in the air and cross on her chest
She tumbled and fell forward
Despite her firm Faith that was so very strong
In a murky puddle of rain water.

82. Faith

A cup of tea remains to be
An everlasting Trinity
Of taste, aroma, soulful ease
Before and after so it seems
Always stays much later on
By far much longer than when
It's gone.
The cuppa comes, relaxes, goes;
Only to surely come back again
In equal vigour, rattling so
As not to fall off from the
Tray- flowery to match the cups.
It's surely worth the wait
And fills with perfect gladness heart
And Soul.
Never doubt it's constant
Worth because it seldom
Leaves us lonely or to
Struggle with our woes
Without the thrill to
Move along with the rising of the sun
Or its setting even so.

83. Smaller Woes

If you haven't showered
Or bathed— it's little less than
Tragedy.
For reasons known-unknown to you
You'll go wrong with all you do
Moody, angry and impolite
All born of the fact that
Timely, you did choose to utterly
Forget—that bathing helps you
Not to sweat.
Remember this for tomorrow
And the next that will
Duly follow. Bathe and shower
Shower and bathe and never
Ever yourself disgrace.
Don't resist
The urge to pee
Or to follow up
Your needs.
As they're the building blocks of life
Take you far, far into life.
If you choose still not to heed

These simple urges
You may breed
A host of difficult
Ills and fevers that shall follow.
For small things that were
Carelessly so for granted taken
Left unattended and neglected:
You've paid a rather heavy price—
Not a penny or a dime
But something else that's so
Divine.
If you love to dress each time
With the changing of the sun
To match yourself with mood and shade
Echoing everything around
You are just then in your cause
So keep going without pause.
Early to bed and early to
Rise
Can do wonders if you try.
The story does not end but here—
Don't be drowsy or upset that
You woke early to prepare
Breakfast and a tidy lunch;
AND…
Then with rattling bunch of keys
To open up with routine care,

Many doors that were bolted right
To stop the thieves from prowling round
In the middle of the night
And last of all the huge red gate
It's time to click the lock that's
Been there for five and twenty
Or more odd years — shinier with age and weather
For all those who did get up
Late.
Madness does to some degree
Aids you with impartiality.
You stop to dwell on petty things
That burden you with the sense
Of worthless time and energy
Spent for nothing real to
Catch or gain.
You never see a man who begs
As someone whom you may
Neglect—
Selfishness in all kinds of garbs
Are unraveled, stark and bare.
This heightened mental state acquires
New abilities; sharp discriminations
And the like.
This is why the common man
Catches, imprisons one that's
Not committed to the race of life.

The mad man faces all the strife.
Think carefully and you will know
The futility that we go through
When in the end it comes to
Nought— whatever may have been the thought.

84. There was once a plump girl

From Wivelsfield Green
Who wore a short dress of
The most horrible sheen
It was purple and white
With flowers and red leaves.
Her braids weren't too long
Or pretty or strong
Come sunshine or hail, she always looked pale
Her teeth were stuck out
But she wasn't a rabbit—I swear,
This ordinary girl of eighteen.
She smiled but not laughed
She stood and not crouched
She was fair and right smooth with earnest blue eyes
That looked very clever;
She had almost and ever
Both hands at the back.
It took quite a while to know who she was
Creative and gay and spending the day
Watching and looking so far far away

Then only one time
When her mother was gone
She made friends with us all and was eager to play.
She could run, jump and win
The others a-spin
But still locked her hands at her pretty young back
She was mirthful and funny
Both Silly and sad in the course of the day
With arms at the back.
Maybe this pose was her magic and strength
That made her the winner
Every time that she played
Her face became brighter
She changed and she grew
Taller than anyone else; faster than few
She still wore her plaits
Oily or not: but bought a new frock
With coins that were rusted and were kept in a bag
Of velvet and lace, resembling a cake
Belonged to her mother through thick and thin weather.
She treasured the bag more than the money all gone
She still liked the colours
Which were purple and black
She married and carried the
Burden along but only grew
Stubborn through wearing and tearing
God save her soul as once she

had been
Slender and single, jumping with beans.
One day they would find
That she'd left in a hurry, taking her bag without any money
Such people are rare but they're certainly there
To tease us, appease us
And leave us behind
To worry and scurry, to cry and to wallow
In the deepest, most dreadful despair.

85. The King of Fruits

I haven't eaten mangoes like
This, believe me when I say:
I'm sick of eating but won't forego
A single one that comes my way.
I remember rainy days of
Youthful rapture, years ago—
My busy doctor-father come
Back home for a lunch and mangoes too
That were indeed an orange colour
Earthy red and yellow bloom.
Coffee followed not too late
— Time to resume a happy
Afternoon.
Each of us delighted with the march of
Time: of the day and of the night.
With the breezy wind and weather
Fragranced rich with rarest
Mangoes meadow-green; sunshine yellow
Honest orange; hectic red; with
A hint of azure blue— blue takes over
Almost everything on earth
It is the law of Nature — sky and

Ocean; water too are all in
The hues of the most earnest
Of all Blues: navy, sky, ocean
Bright subdued; porcelain and glassy too
Classic jeans and denim; tent- house blue
And True… the list goes on
And many are yet to take their names
But for just now this is good
Enjoy the mangoes while you can!

86. The Edge

Man will struggle to be not
At the center but at the edge
Of everything and everywhere
He does find himself.
The center is a space that has
Turned into a wretched hole
That sucks into your mind and
Heart before you know that you're
Stuck into a place so far away
From everything that you have
Sworn.
The center is a dismal place
It's dark and narrow, stifling too,
To carry on with eagerness and the spirit of Abandon .....
Don't go too far into the middle
Go return to breezier winds
Where you may walk a mile or two
Without infecting one another.
The edge may speeden up your
Fall onto the other side that's nought
And hurls you into a space that
Dangles you much far you

May ever imagine that it can do.
It has its pitfalls too you know
Sometimes with unmeasured
Trips of complicatedness.
But one thing you may be interested in
Is the vastness of the dip
And indifference of the cavern
Withholding all the fright and passion;
Of what exactly got you there. So take the chance to look on in
To the other Realm beyond.

Words of Wisdom

Wisdom and age are not necessarily companions. Wisdom may not come at the end… Wisdom is born out of intensity of – feeling, thought and sensitive interpretations.

87. Music

Music of a different
Kind can be heard now
That you grow old—
Listen to the unknown beats;
The caress of the winds that
Blow and to the Even song.
Sights look different at the End
Hues and trees and buildings
Too. Vague yet bright and dark
But glowing in a sacred, Hallowed Light. Don't feel sad or shaken
Up in what seems a desperate hour:
It's just like there's the Setting Sun
And tomorrow rises on the banks
Of Faith and Goodness everywhere.

88. Grow Old

Yeats' thoughts of growing
Old together have been
Taught to generations to the
Young, ambitious people of
The classroom listening to
An unknown, forgotten phase
Of Life that doesn't really
Ring true— it's miles if not Eons
Away— who cares for Oldies
Anyway.
However much the young
Aspire and know that Age
Is far away
The imprint of the image that Yeats so aptly gave—
The burning of the fireside to
Keep both warm; hand-in-hand
And see each other till the
End of Time.
Stays till it's time to say good-bye.

89. Missing Goa

I thought I'd miss the awesome sea
The wind and wave and road
And trees. The ball of fire going down
The whistling of the summer ghosts
Through autumnal leaves.
The turns the twists, the bumps,
The folk, the people full of shadowed
Glee..the pubs and pizzas,
Cars and hookahs; mini skirts
And Birkenstocks— Beach ware
Shops in much the same,
Mimicry and antique lays;
Flying over all around.
I'm back again and true belong,
To this the place—Jaipur is the name;
Where I do stand..
It's quite a shift, I understand
And also do perceive, that I
Will never miss the place I'm
Talking of, for now; just in this moment
Realise, I brought it back with me
Forever. In a hundred different ways

My life is fragranced from the touch
Of such Divinity.

90. An Eagle Attack

Unexpected is a word
Full right we follow what it may be
And know how much it may befall
IN
A hundred ways and
In a hundred means.
And yet, the Unexpected, does not teach
Us to prepare, for so many invisible
Corners near and far: Other stranger, unperceived
Shadows, so as to be aware:
Lurking on and growing; in whatever Space
And Time they duly prosper in.
Thinking of the ravages of storms and earthquakes too:
Tsunamis and volcanic threats; with minds full of
The obvious— of Terrorist attacks; we forget the deadly Rodent
Squirming at our feet, or the hissing Snake unheard;
And there behold some dangling Branch
Falls on your head to strike you down;
Think again to wonder.. beware of all around.
Don't expect the unexpected
To frame your thoughts, however wild
It goes beyond itself always—

It is the nature of God's things.
Allow yourself to think beyond
You will be better off you know:
Consider all the things you don't:
Like fire in the water or, an iceberg
In the blazing summer heat... better still,
Connect, to what's around—
What lies ahead, to which, you never can and never will.
Whoever thought of Eagles wild,
Who are the masters of the sky,
To look upon your lovely head
From some distance jealously...
Knowing only to attack, it swoops
So wickedly; brushes past — leaving you
Bewildered. Amazed and shocked
A sensual and a soul attack.
In nightmares that do follow day,
You'd think of this and that..
But never ever turned your mind, to this unique,
Dreadful Monarch of the skies.
What had you done to live this day,
Where you stand dumb aghast ,
Slight knowledge of the Brute that's simply
Wicked, wild...
A timely thought yet does occur—
It could have been much worse:
Fury might have led the bird to ravage you

Once more: the second time so horrible
It well could be a curse—unknown,
Unfathomed fetched: from the deepest shores
Of cunning Hebrides…
Or some such woes that come to us
In love or labour; who knows, from both!
In haste and knowledge you look up all
Banks of information—to track this somewhat
Unfortunate, unusual event—Many explanations; many data
Show the way to understanding of the thing that
Passed your path today—the head still muddled, hurt from
The blow that was received, will have a memory
Now forever, of its very own.
However much all other fears take over:
Swarming long your head and heart, a dear and stern,
Kind whispering voice will help erase this time,
Together with rewards, that may only help to
Reach, the heights where Eagles fly.

91. Dreamy Realities

I love to find connections in the light of day
Of what happens in my dreams
In the darkness of the night.
This happens seldom all because
Forgotten are the dreams I have
Remembering still the sea of thought and feeling
That it always brings along.
Sometimes there are distant though distinct
Resemblance of what went on
In the dreamy song that hits one
In a sudden jerk or evanescence of a lucid
Moment.
Some dreams gain focus and are stable
Each detail does outspend its time
Forever gaining ground with
Brilliance of the motions it gracefully makes
Towards the return of some precious Moments.
So if you are able to connect to
Something to the daylight from
The passing of last night— the
Blessing's there; hold it tight
And make the most of what you have.

92. The Familiar

So accustomed do we get
To what's familiar day to day
That all that's gone is not at all
Good enough—all that's to come
Is to be despised; no matter
What such state does mean,
We'll cling onto the dreams
We have; letting go is thrust
Upon sans joys of changes
Come upon from above or
From the shuffling of the crowd
That does outdo the stagnant
Ground to displace the other
Into the second of the space.

93. Present-Day Goblins

Goblins have always been around
In the woods or forests where
They build their nasty little
Dwellings, hatching plans to ruin
Men and women; children fair.
By hook, by crook—through sheer disguise; Patience
Laughter, fun and wile…
They struggle still till all is
Lost—and when gained ground,
They loud proclaim, their truth
Of wickedness and foul intent…
All smiles turn into awful gnarls. After capturing
Your soul, your trust, your faith in them; they then begin their nasty game
Of killing off your inhibitions; turning wild your gentleness;
On the brink of toxic state, where nothing, no-one
Does remain, of any worthwhile consequence!
It's not for you to put the blame on him or her or anyone:
Neither GOBLINS nor those DRUGS, or fancy coloured liquids served,
In mesmerising shapes of bottles shining forth the crystal glass,
Are to be single blamed. Remind yourself that POISON is,

Mostly marked by BEAUTY still; to mislead all who
Are willing; curious, weak, and ever-ready, glad to always be misled.
Those are the ones who somehow would be glad to be in
Trouble and to be, oh so much as mis-under-stood.
Don't give yourself the double CREDIT for being naive
And toxic too, and blame forever wicked GOBLINS for
Showing you the path to DOOM.
Remember this and all is FAIR:
You yourself did hunt them down;
Existence only bore the CROWN
The concept born was in your own
True jumbled MIND.
From EARTH to EARTH is an all-time LAW;
Suck back DESIRE that's made you FALL.
The Goblins of your fine-meshed mind are far more
Dangerous than them, who somewhere in the woods
And forests, lighting fires, cooking up,
Nasty plans for human beings, who have as much
Been nasty too—
Enough, as you have noticed now, invented—
Viruses and Atom Bombs.

94. The Ugly Duckling: A Pub

What's in a name: nothing else
But everything.
The globe itself is
All about names before
Any other thing that rolls
Or stays or goes.
Your name is yours
Begged borrowed stolen
It is not.
Likewise is the name that's there
On every object place or thing.
It's not a static thing at all
It changes with the moving of
Time and space;
That we always have at hand.
Needless to say, the world would be
Without these names a darkened
Place; a perfect mess.
The Ugly Duckling is eternal
In my heart—its name is what

Amused me first-the yellow sketch;
The pink and pouting rounded beak;
The emblem of a childhood friend.
Our friendship grew; it was the first
I'd greet on my morning way to
School. It stood aloft a banner tall
Serving as a lamppost too, when the
World was turning dark.
I'd find it smiling all the time
When on return my willing feet
My heart quite warm and bathed
From friends and teachers there
In school, from playing, learning
One big balloon—my little yellow
Constant friend, winking in the
Light that twilight soon would become.
I grew up and life became somewhat
Different; I now would glance at other
Things and cared to venture: looked inside
With bated breath and tremblings
Inside the place—woe the day!
That little Duckling stood there for.
At first it was the smoke and shouts
That made me somewhat crazy, scared
An ugly weave of smoke and sound I'd
Never seen or heard—At the most
My father's pipe we found such comfort in

And friendly, lively little cans of good old
British beer, honestly,
Was all I'd ever seen.
I felt sorry that my friend—the little
Yellow gentle Duckling, without
His mother all around, unassuming, uncomplaining,
Was made to stay and advertise an awful place
That no good man would allow himself
To go. What business had these strange,
Pathetic human beings, to lift a name
From out of holy, untouched pure,
Children's books to glorify their messy
Chaos that they'd built?
I would think ahead of time—
If ever was a sin so bad;
It was of sneaking innocence to fit
The glove, of a measly little dirty hand.

95. A Radical Thought

A premonition is a dangerous, alarming, jumpy thing
As child I often wondered—always asked:
People who were stronger, elder, about the
Horror of such thing as knowing what was not, but yet
To be, and the awful idea that something told us
Through signs or irregular beatings of the heart,
Just how and when it ought to be.
The distance between the thought and done
Could well be wide or very narrow; that wasn't though,
My real or only sorrow: I hated still the very thought
And asked my Dad again, again—"This means to me the horrible
Truth that the deed will then the thought, surely always follow. If this is fact
Then woe the day; what then do we have a Free Will for?"
To which my Dad pretended: not to understand— "Go on silly girl—
Get rid of all your doubts and play, just like any other girl your age!"
Even surer than before—I let myself burst into a song
I knew for sure that I had asked, a question only few would dare,

Knowing well that science and philosophy combined together, with their
Wondrous antitheses, (metaphysics) had found a Clue of what I'd said,
About the thought before the deed; An explanation only one,
Amongst many more unknown to me: Or any other—
That, Premonition only means, that you can never, ever
Be the writer of your human life alone, with Will or Faith that things
Turn out, better braver if you're cautious and controlled. There is something that moves along
In strongest bearing yet, not identified: over which you or I
Have no control—Maybe that's what we name, our 'Destiny.'

96. If Indeed

If I could fly like I could walk
I don't think I would
Take the pain; for profit
Or for any other gain.
For what you have is never enough
It's always sad, it's always tough—
We're wanting always what is not.
Thinking, working all in vain
Enjoy the journey again they said—
It's all a gift this human life
Full of sweetness, full of light.
It's something that you have today
Tomorrow will be turning
Into another day and yet
Who knows when and how it does
The act of not receiving.
For here and
For evermore.
If I could sing like a nightingale
I'd want no more
To do with spring. All the music that I'd have,
Would spread across the oceans

Bling!
If there is calm before the storm
Then let the peace come through
Right after the riot of winds and clouds
Let it be peaceful too.
What's good for one
Is good for you
I just so realized
That we'd lived our lives
And thought this wasn't true.

97. Listen

Turn again Dick Whittington
Thrice Lord Mayor of London
This certain does now ring a bell
And serves as a constant guide
To merely this that it conveys
Do not spare yourself of this
Where signs and madness
Teaches you to listen to that extra sound— the voice of
Prophecy that's present even in the humble call of chiming
Church bells or the voices in the
Street— or nodding heads of
Pica lilies by the sidewalk
Or the gully.
It's the voice of your own heart
That's externalised in all around
So that you find the
Final answer of the best and most
Superior, restless agitation.
Lose
Your heart to the wind that
Blows; the flowers that bloom
Or are drooping low. Give in to the

Many Gifts of Man and God
Who both do strive onto the path
Of only this— that we should be
Inspired, alive and integrated
With what is therein Harmony with Symphony.

98. By the Time

It's never too late to begin anew
To start again from scratch right through
We've been told so often now
Reflection does but only show
That:
By the time we fold our hands in gratitude
Thank the Lord for every little gift He's given
To count our blessings;
Tempted: not to ever, with much greed
Peep into another's waving, luscious greenest fields;
To wonder, stretch and live
Anew, every single sunny day.
By the time
We've rightly managed to scrimp and save and struggle through
Life's unexpected turns and halts
To dry our clothes when duly washed
To finish off with undone work
And heave a sigh of big relief;
By the time we've tidied up
And loved and lost and grieved
Forgot... the pain to start afresh
By the time life closes in with gay abandon, frolic, fun...

Newer, louder sunrise; crimson , golden sunsets;
Great insights and new perceptions;
Lovely hues of fresh awareness
Like the colours of the rainbow.
By the time we've quite Achieved
Our heart's desires and much more—
Mastered baking and the arts;
Driving, saving, hosting, loving
Playing chess or shearing hedges
As we then have travelled far
Another country, culture clime
To find solace in some other
Unknown and unexplored —Unexpected, Space of Time:
Come back once more and
Stayed and knew the value
Of the smaller, more familiar,
Things.
By the time we've much discovered
The secrets of our precious lives
Eager to retrieve and gain
What was lost along the way
It's time to move to other realms
Where solitude does reign supreme
Or what wonders, what strange sights
Are looming large and bright within
That other space— the
Awesome magic there beyond

Blank and bare to write along
Another story that revolves round
And round another song
Of human wonders and endeavours
Rising, seizing and then depleting.
A circle never really full— it's mastered the supremest art
Of never ending; moving on.

99. Drink your tea while it's still hot

Live your day most of the time
Conscious, happy full
Of caution
Sip as slowly like you would.
Relish it for taste, aroma and effect
Till the bottom of the cup
Then put it down for a just pause
To ponder, wonder, and all that.
Put your feet full on the
Ground: feel the texture, touch or warmth
Tell yourself that you're alive
Hale and hearty; fit and fine.

Last Few Years

The best usually happens in the last hours of your struggle…the truth comes to light; pieces fall into place.

100. A Gift: My Students

I hate to go I'd love to stay
To pray and love all those around
With my easy gait and mood
Accomplished after losing ground
On many scores of God knows
What.
Not every day may I meet those
Whom I have loved so tenderly…
Their Image is embedded such
As fast into the rock, the gem refusing to detach
Or is the morning to the sun;
And night-time all of moon and stars.
Who may tear away these pairs
Such lies in earthly love affairs
Sons and daughters widespread are
In classrooms textbooks pages rare
We've had the best— Gods be praised
So that I don't never ever
Miss them like it's done or like nevermore.

101. The Last Warning

One thought of money in such terms
That money could outdo, many wrongs
Done unto us by life and others all alike.
It was true for half of many centuries
Till in a moment the earth was shattered
On account — a deadly, mean and much alive
Smallest atom-like in shape and size;
Virus that so much now is a part, of our torn-apart and wretched lives.
Out went the wealth of millions across
The globe to disappear with none gone a-missing
Or creating of a vacant place. All thoughts
Of profit, glamour, or of power that could be bought
With digits in your bank, were meaningless
If there were no other man or woman you would meet
On the road across. Social distancing; no parties;
Glamour in-between; no-one looking much
Beyond their own long noses and rough hands.
Masks have altered how we look—dramatically so;
One would hardly know oneself, if shown suddenly the
Familiar, now unfamiliar, half-hidden visage—
Vanity replaced by fear of losing what we have.

Cosmetics better thrown away—clothes and objects elaborate
Show hideous signs of melting into black and sticky tar.
Art along with written words have proved the echo of the
Lines that Shakespeare wrote in faith that
Eternity lives on, not in lifeless monuments that are
'Besmeared with sluttish Time,'
But in honest, fair poetry's, tenderly expressed,
Refreshed eternal lines.
In such case all gathered so, fancy items could remain
For a much longer stay;
It might come out that they'd still provide
For pleasure on a rainy day.
Indifferent children close at hand; Spouses have
Postponed their plans to separate; as life may
Sooner take away the presence of the unwanted other,
Who in eternal absence will fondly prove quite otherwise:
Absence makes the heart grow fonder.
The court and Judge will have their dubious ways
But the virus shoots the very mark it sets eye
On first of all. No choices really do remain
At the end of a long, merciless, infested Corona Day.
It seems it's never going away for
Good. This Demi-God has seized the world
To turn the tables over on what's been around
That should have not. Our pride in what we gave ourselves
Science, technology; will not survive the blows of
Such Fate, that's offered thus.

It's like returning to a home that
Caught fire too suddenly; when you were happily
In the carefree business of routine and every day. Lo behold,
If at all you're back, the embers of the precious
Place leave you much beyond the horror of it all.
The pain is intense; cannot comprehend—
Follows with the rubbing of tear-dry eyes; of
Failed hands that have now to just let go.
A perfect blank is all we have and have been slyly
Offered: the painful, unwelcome, saddest freedom
To take up Pen and rewrite steady, the stories of our lives again.
Do we have the gumption or the daring spirit
To write out pages where the ink may disappear
Even before the thought that's finished. Struggling,
Sighing at the sight: the one that's broken bit by bit
Into a million smithereens?
Does this not remind us of the haughty
Cruel Queen, who wouldn't want another to look beautiful and gay?
And when her wicked mirror shattered at the strike of nought,
Utterly destroyed forever, her love for self and despise for else
Ending on a grimmest note of nevermore.
What we knew is well behind: our hearts and
Minds are jumbled up like a garish kaleidoscope of many
Coloured patterns but with no clear lines or shapes to follow
The path of where we're all, lining up to go.
All sense asleep and yet awake to the misfortunes

This has brought. It seems not that this present state
Has a death in store. It is partial for itself like such entities have been
Always overshadowed by superior self-esteem.
The future of us, we fellow men, is just a hollow echo
Where no sound really responds to a clear background
To something that's really nothing at all: not there.
If today we figure out the mystery that often lies,
Behind such grave and dire cosmic happenings;
We may at least pause a simple moment, to honestly regret
Our base and singular, often selfish, cruel human activities.
In fact, undoubtedly this all falls, in line with human
Greed of many different kinds; pride and prejudice...senselessness
Thrashing out so readily at others' dignity. Selfish to the core—
A monstrous Greed for almost every other thing that glitters
All around.
Mother Nature's gentle, firm and loving
Stern, corrective Hand; a whip, a lashing cutting
Through the stubborn layers of what we've wrought:
Hopefully to kindly, resurrect, a rotting human race.
But early not to think—
In punishment of such cosmic kind, we cannot
Wish for just rewards—of bringing back to human
Life those who lost the battle... but indeed a prayer
In consciousness of the blessed Earth that gives us life;
A promise made unto ourselves of gaining back
Our hard, honest, sacred sanctity of caring and of giving;

Of the thought before the leap; for others too. The daring and the Devil
Who's never too far behind in awful strategy.
Nothing was ever given to one Human alone; Luck may come and go
With the fleeting of the moment; what remains is the
Vast unknown, the petty done, the constant state that
Never leaves—misery, mortality, hunger, pain
And the final fatality, of unsightly, inhuman Vanity.

102. Tears

Tears are such a seldom thing
They are now a precious act
Of pure transparent crystal
Thought. Without the burden
Of how to gain
Or selfish sprinklings of the fact
That boundless chase fears
Away to bring back feelings
Of a long-forgotten comfort
In the whiteness- virgin state.

103. Darkest before Dawn

I am not yet too very old but seek forgiveness
From other humans busy as the bees. For one thing I've
discovered now— exact this moment
Of writing down… and now forgotten…
Help me please, my mind speeds on
With wretched ease: I hope it's not
The blackened darkness before another
Kind of dawn. I think you know:
Or the glow or melting fast
Retiring candle just like me.

104. The Summit

I was dazzled by the sounds and the bellows
Of the blowing Breeze and the rising of the Sun.
I marked it off for something Grand and lived quite long in firmest Faith.

I was dazzled by the Man who lived next door with wealth and health.
I marked it off as something Grand and did endeavour all day long
To gain whatever was.

I was dazzled by many people
I came across as all too neat; Prim and proper always Grand
In speech and gestures; proud and strong.

I was drowned in sensuous Awe, of horse and man together,
Speeding steady over the Downs; across the ponds
Into the town; with grace and passion yet unknown.

The beauty of a dark brown Mare, wrapped up in frenzy
Of the wild — wild wind that blew about

In truthful echo of what the horse must honest feel.
Was this a point in time that had held onto the Truth divine-
Of the oneness of it all, locked in ragged Unity
Of motion and in gleeful, heavy, rhapsody.

I was dazed, spellbound indeed A Mare that was trapped inside
Beside, her own frenzied, Untamed joys; a bellyful of Primitive
Fears, the rawness hurting deep inside.

I look elsewhere to ease the pain
Of Passion of extreme degree
I wish for balance in the motion Of the firm but gentle; meek and mild;
Rocking of the cradle.
And beauties at the sight of Babies nourished from the breast.
Or being born and then progressing…
To run the even race of men.

I was dazzled always
Anew, with God's marvels- multitude…
Like the infinity of the sea; the cat the dog in enmity; the milk the maid;
The pretty young girl who sat in a chair;
The windy boy who ran across the road so bare.

I looked around for many more

Till the linnet sang its Song
I spent precious years to arrive And understand, when all marvels disappeared,
The only marvel left untapped was
That special marvel which was me.
In our Quest for other things
We lose ourselves in our retreat
From the chance to rediscover
A universe that's trapped inside, waiting it does seem forever.

I now do stand upon the peak of sunset mountain;
Rich and rare the air does seem;
Laden, ripe, with bygone times and fulfilled dreams.
I look around; I stand alone; I do not hear the sound
Of almost anything. So still, Profound is this pure state
Of watching now—grateful but lost to the blank.
Deep the reds and purples are that close in on most everything
Preparing for the final round or maybe just to so begin
Another day: familiar motions earnest sounds.
Whatever it is that takes the place; I'm pretty sure
Of the trust, of the care and of Abundance of the Lord.

I alone do stand and face, the measured breeze that seems so
Slow: to gather speed. No, it will not.
The only other sound I hear— is the Red inside my chest:

The beatings rhythmic; all too Loud, to be missed forever now.
For the first time i do listen to a sound I've never ever
Heard before—
It is the steady, flowing, sure,
Muffled thuddings of my heart—
I look down in appeal and find: a microcosm living there.

It's never too late it's never too wrong
To know what's not or who forgot
To use that Only, golden chance;
For always round the corner there
Will be another bend—
Where the beginning and the end;
In Trust and Friendship fair;
Will surely meet to join again.

105. Alternatively

The sailing ships for reaching
Home is now a myth
In memory. Admirals and
Pirates; stormy weather;
Battles won or lost; are now indeed
Part and parcel of a far-flung Past.
They sail for entertainment now
And give some mimic fun.
Roller coaster fun and fare
Squealing boys and glummest
Men have the thrills of the
Monster-like machine.
Life no more has such fun or daring.
Gathering objects; loading on
To beautify a life not there
It's time to turn the clock around
And ramble through the treasures of the
Wide expanse that Nature offers
Without a tag
Without a price
Take and leave
Whatever you want.

106. A Meltdown

Mergers happening everywhere
I sometimes wonder what they're at
Growing wide and wider still
Or self-containing paradox.
It's hard to tell and others too
Are taking trend of merging
Through so that a faceless
Mass is formed— take it leave it
As you will. This denies a faithful, trusted
Overlap of seamless borders
Wade along without attachment,
Features, pride, they now
Belong to a forgotten territory
If remembered, it's called,
The PAST.

107. So Far and no Further

No one looks out of the window
No one holds open the door
For letting someone in to have
A Quiet cup of tea and more.
Windows barred; doors shut tight
Even the wind does heave a sigh
And dodges places that do hide.
Children playing as they did
Are rare to see or listen to.
Youthful maids and daring
Men, are both hidden from the
World at large.
Grandma, Grandpa and my uncle
All are huddled up inside the space
Between one wall and the next
In confinement from the rest
Of us to escape the fatal
Germ-filled Breeze outside.
Think of the time when it will
Come— when the world goes back
To what it used to be. With spirits low
With passive mind, indifference and apathy

The body in a limp and totter
Fumbling for just so surviving
The unknown face and rigours
Of the time we call Today.
The past has lost its glamour too
The present is a gift that has
A life today— tomorrow morn
It may just be, the very very end.
The future is the moment next
No vision of the distant destination
Or great plans on growing old,
Raising happy your children's children
Who are of course, your very own.
We find great solace and friendship too
In our tables, books and chairs;
The food we cook or clean the stairs
It's in the little oddest tasks
That brings delight to mind and heart.
All clothes are one; we want to wear
Without a reason or a place to
Visit neither here nor there.
The Malls are shut with cobwebs fine
Theatre is a thing quite of the past; a memory of bygone days
And medieval chivalry.
Schools go deadly quiet without
The beatings of the morning drum
The earnest crunchy march past done, or

Of children's bitter-happy screeching cries.
Teachers shouting, Be in line
Chins up chest out and
Stomach in!!
Streets are wanton wanting
Wear from hurried feet and
Gleaming trams to rumble
Through the ground without
A care. People yawning,
Shifting, Smiling into nothing
Or in despair, of having courage to
Be out, to work, in hitting hail or sinful shine.
Online classes; online wares
No good things to laugh about or the story bright to share.
Save the tip tip of the phone
Facebook Facetime WhatsApp
Too.
Growing duller by the hour
Feeling tired without the sweat
Or gruelling schedule of the office
Or the eagerness to spend just
Another extra hour…
No delight of opening the door
After an interesting fun filled day
To the return of Him who earns the bread
For family and all who
Live under the expanded, widened

Roof.
The doors are shut against all
Time. Nothing extra but the din
Of the house and wash machine.
The landline lies forgotten there
On the dusty shelf that's bare;
Voices on the phone are rare
Too much effort is required to talk to someone
Longing for, people places and some things
When nothing's happened
For so long.
Repeat yourself yet every day
And think of yourself as still
Just living the way, you did
With overdues of every sort
Stepping out to finish chores
Or going to and fro from
School, building up a future for
Your little child or grown-up Teen.
The day is done in quite a jiffy though,
The mind just helps combat the
Haze of one day running, into the light of the next
With open windows; open doors—
Be careful everyone; you need to
Remember to shut tightly, each and every one.

Uncanny

When the uncommon grazes against the common, is when man experiences another realm of awareness.

108. A Puff of Cloud: A Premonition

If you're halted in the midst of going for a walk
Into the woods, or for buying useless stuff
In mindless boredom or retreat;
Inside a big and senseless Mall,
And sudden you should see, no one or no other thing,
But an instant puff of cloud that bursts ahead
And fast ascends, the highest peaks of Amsterdam;
And if in one such crazy moment, it is gone to
Puff again after ten steps taken; twenty they could also be:
And dog your path in front and not behind—be sure to know
Your dearest one is in serious trouble—rush away before 'tis late
It may have been already.
Such signs are rapid, unexpected;
But exist as always, in some or other form
In the hollows of the pockets of the yellow Air:
Of knowledge that we don't yet have but may acquire
Soon or late to know how, when and why there are
The untold secrets of the world.

109. Not Absent

Death did confirm yet once again,
That it always was at large,
It visited— a secret meet—
Where dreamt I,
On and on and on.
My father died some bad twelve years
Ago—I've lived with this in pain of parting
Much forever; and in pleasant memories
That make things evermore,
Without the option to touch or see
The dear one once again.
But why should this, but in a dream
Come back so clear to me… as if
The pain was wearing off and it was
Once again, a time to think and
Feel the pain of parting so once more,
Lest I drowned in ignorance or
Think that Time conspires, to
Good forget the awful doom of
Man and beast together gone:
One day would come to all.
The dream… The same grey day of rain and black

Sky and clouds all gathered there
As was the day we talk about,
Entrenched in memory so vivid,
'Twas more real than e'er before
Or on the day it really happened.
They say that truth is harsh and rough;
That nothing else is worse; but
I proclaim, all very well, that dreams
Are sure no better— they add on
Grief and lots of sorrow in a realm
That's worse to be… a nightmare yet indeed!
Marches, runs, skips and jumps; so back and forth; so mad
And sad; hurried in a cloudy state:
Confusion as to what came first and what was second;
The laws of this, the world of dreams
Are many: but a few of them will
Pin you down to follow what's
In the living world:
In gaiety or in Piety—
Believe me it's a world
That shows, much more than
Many any.
Do not conclude what you have seen
As to have given whole a thing;
You do not know, what round the
Bend, awaits for good discovery:
Recognition, interpretation, calculus or integration.

The factor X will good be there
To surprise in continuation.

110. Horror

No one else was free to visit the dearest
Heiress to this large and sprawling Bungalow:
A little shattered, weird and hollow—
If that makes sense to all who follow
The words and lines of this, the present Tale.
The heiress of a Baron proud—the meek and strong
Fair Earbenstein, for long long hours
She wrote inside, with many pages white, some yellow,
Here within the Dark and Dreary, battered room; dried-up flowers
Hanging from the walls and windows; ceiling too,
Never the light to once behold or the wind to naturally blow.
No poetry or no prose she wrote
That anyone really knows about
A constant scribbling with laughs and tears
She engaged herself for hours.
These constant sounds had fast become
The background of the biggest house
In all of picturesque Easterdom.
People knew but wouldn't tell
Or talk about the special powers
That undoubtedly, she true possessed.

For who would write and write and write
Till hours had spent all minutes, seconds that they had --
The count of twenty-four or more?
How she lived and what she ate and drank inside
The room, to keep alive—is unknown, till this very day.
Spirits of a special sort were companions of her own kind—
Would talk to her in quiet whispers
Sometimes even loud aloud
Depending on the wish and time
Provided by the Spirit tender.
Known unknown would gather there
Spirits from actually everywhere
Happy sad and sometimes vengeful of an unpredicted kind
She'd befriended most of them
But lost all who waited outside
The door, with no voice to ever respond.
Relatives, friends, neighbours, all did think
Giving up was a darn good thing—
'To each his own' must be followed
In word and spirit now and then.
She was special, vague and absent, dearest Earbenstein— she spun out
Tales of these dear and awful spirits; troubled, mad and deeply sad.
In writing out their wishes bold
Through her power of words and keenest Art;

It was great service to an unknown territory of souls like
ourselves, and yet
Not fully so—In this they then would find release
To express themselves; and in so doing,
Forget, forgive their own, and others' sins; Redress
The deadly wounds and woes, of lost loves or of petty goals.
Forgiveness does the soul release, one's own as well as
Others'; Embittered, maybe dead, maybe alive
Now; long-forsaken Earthly foes.

111. The Spell

It was as if some hidden thing
Was moving everywhere
From home to town the whole
Way long; not ready to leave without
Doing something that was to be
Done. Cautious, sneaky; very
Very sly, dogmatic. Dodging traffic
Absent ditches, visible witches
People beggars but this one
Didn't give a clue as to who he
Was or what to do.
It wasn't till after the deed was
Done — leaving us bewildered
Sober to the point of unknown pain.
Reality turned into a spell that
Left us fumbling for ourselves
When the car swerved past the gates—
The only home I've ever known before
I built my very own.
We'd driven into town for need of buying things
For easing out, Dull domestic chores.
I knew the house in front of me

Would make my heart miss many beats
It nearly stopped when we were made
To park it right in front of our dear
Father's garage door — the door
That held shut very stubborn very tight
in its own rightful place —
Refusing to open now to let in anyone
Who may appear to be his master's
Friend, foe or just another passing man.
The absent force that sailed us there
Was he an angel or a demon?
Who stood aloft both door and car; to witness the encounter.
Was he a friend or enemy
Hard to tell it was just now.
The feeling that we both did have
In this moment of both despair and reunion of whatever sort
Does defy the written or the spoken word.
As human beings we look always
For some or other explanation
Of what goes on when we have lost
All reason and do find ourselves
In distant and forgotten lands
Where all the spheres will congregate to conjure up and Then
create a place familiar and at the same time
Very rare.
The harmony of unknown souls
Living here or existing, in some other

Heavenly Realm.
Whatever the energies that move behind
Such extra dimensional, special territory
Does not really matter when
The end brings together thus
A long-lost soul to justly
Gaze on such special, archetypal, home once theirs.

112. Conquered Fears

I lost all fear of stupid ghosts
When noises like a tapping
Or of scuffling took silent hold
Of the empty space— my house
I have revisited for something
Good to do.
Ghosts have been my only fear
Since when I've been so very small
They've changed all shape and size you
Know, according to the age I am.
This rather big and evil rat (maybe a rodent)
Hugged itself so that I barely saw it
Slithering past against the edge
Of the humble corridor— I believe that
It had jumped straight on from the window ledge!!
I thought of all my fine, old-new clothes;
My pages crafted in moments of creativity
Degrees and files scattered here there
Everywhere!!
Although the interview was done; why should
I allow a mean fat rat to destroy my life's
Endeavours just for fun?!

Have mercy oh you nasty creatures
We can never match your potent powers
Or your speed and high intense, smells
Of food or human beings.
I know you also have dear life
As equal to any other; I won't kill you
I'd feel sad and guilty for as long—
I cannot bring myself to craft a
Bucket full of water or a DIY to
Cheat you; trick you; throw you
Out!!!!
I have found a method though
Sans violence (swear) of any kind
That respects you as a host to
An unwanted guest: I'll block
Your grand way back into my little
Humble precious-poor: vacant
Home sweet Home.
Just like folks fast block the people
They don't like or want around;
On logs or WhatsApp, Facebook more:
It's easier than blocking you, y'know.
One last word in thankfulness
To you for making me rid my horrible
Fears (of ghosts) you know;
As I could clamber dig and dive
All through the lonely darkest night!!

No, I will ne'er forget that night
I'll mark it off as one unique
With the lightning and the thunder
Furious howling desperate wind
Rattling at the loosened doors
And windows: me with all my might
And courage— confronting one
I'd barely see!!

Epilogue

I do not wish to summarize the proceedings of the verses in this book. Summaries usually tend to conclude... and conclusions for me are irrelevant as there are none. I am happy to continue with writing from observation and experience with newer, brighter or subtler shades of understanding. The following two poems in this "Epilogue" refer to the state of feeling overwhelmed with views, images and words and the conflicting desire to continue with my writing. Creativity (writing) has an innate tendency to express itself despite the many kinds of hurdles on the wonderful journey.

Until the next time!

I write, I wrote, I've written

Out for far far too long: I wish for friends to stop me
Now: or I'll be trapped forever more…
In the writing of the song
In many now outnumbered ways..
I cannot stop and maybe not, as possessed I
Truly am.
Should I laugh or should I cry?
Should I blame the genes that dyed
The body, soul and fingers, always searching
Newer words; in order or disorder so,
Fast meandering like the stream—

Looking here and there; many single ways to:
Recreate a thought!
I know this as a blessing rare—do I deserve to sit aglow,
I sit now humbled 'neath a shower of:
Extremest loveliness..
To know to feel and then bring forth
In rapturous multitude…A passing melody:
A song. Thank thee Muse to move along.

Requesting

One major fear to overcome
I admit I have to deal with
This one thing and then
Gently pass away.
Lord give me what I'd rather do
The time enough to write and
Write till writing is no more
My need— I'm happy that I just gave back
Some of what I was so gifted with
Not my own but Nature's course
Of measuring out the length and breadth
Of my humble life's course for me
One last wish if ever granted
If ever soul had voice to say
A few lines in honour of some
Unfinished thought or heart

Let it be the voice of love through
Idiom that lives so close to me.
If granted this an eternal promise
That I would go my proper way
And songs of hurt and mirth would
Follow in the language I have learnt.
Grim forebodings I do have
In pensive and in gloomy mood
That I may lose what I have earned
Let English be the voice I keep
In the soundless cosmic sleep.

Printed by Libri Plureos GmbH in Hamburg,
Germany